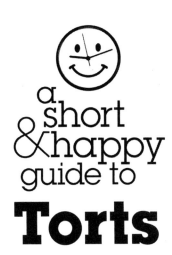

a short & happy guide to Torts

By **Roger E. Schechter**

Professor of Law
George Washington University Law School

WEST®

A Thomson-Reuters business

MAT# 41187564

610 Opperman Drive
Eagan, MN 55123
1-800-313-9378

Printed in the United States of America.

ISBN: 978-0-314-27787-9

For Erica, Bob and Steve . . .
Thanks for all the fish.

Table of Contents

Chapter 4 - Negligence: The Breach Element

Chapter 5 - Negligence: Factual Causation

Chapter 6 - Negligence: Proximate Cause

Chapter 7 - Negligence: Damages

Chapter 8 - Defenses to Negligence Claims

Chapter 9 - Strict Liability For Defective Products

Chapter 10 - Other Strict Liability Claims

Chapter 11 - Dignitary, Economic and Other Torts

Chapter 12 - Vicarious Liability and Other Miscellaneous Topics

INTRODUCTION

1. What This Book Isn't

This book isn't a substitute for going to class or reading the opinions in your casebook. Really. I am not just saying that because the other law professors will beat me up if I don't. I mean it.

Only by going to class will you be able to figure out what your professor thinks is important. Only by reading the cases will you be able to get a sense of how courts formulate and justify legal rules, and what kinds of arguments are considered valid or persuasive by folks in the legal system.

2. What This Book Is

So what is the purpose of this book, if not to spare you the effort of going to class and reading your assignments? Simply put, my goal is to give you some sense of certainty and structure about the material. In order to do the fun stuff—make arguments and critique the legal rules—you need to know what those rules are. While you may be able to deduce the rules from the cases and from class discussion, I have been in the law professor game long enough to know that it is not a sure bet.

Some teachers simply dislike rules so much that they deliberately obscure them. Others are so—what is the word I am looking for here—cerebral, that they are incapable of summarizing the rules. Still others are so mesmerized by the arcane theories they have set out in law review articles that they choose to devote all their class time to those theories rather than to any coverage of the rule structure. It is therefore quite possible for you to get to the end of your first semester without a clear sense of the underlying rule structure in the law of torts. I hope that this book will be a very efficient and very painless antidote to that problem.

Let me put that another way. This book is like a map. It is not a substitute for going on the journey, but my hope is that it will make the journey more efficient and less frustrating. You can turn to it when you get lost and hopefully quickly get back on the path.

3. A Word About Torts

Torts is a cool subject. Of course I'm biased, but it really is. Every society has to have some way of dealing with the problem of injuries. The considerations to be taken into account in designing that system are fascinating. Even more good news is that the cases are entertaining and highly memorable. You cannot believe how many different ways people have come up with to hurt themselves and others.

That said, most law students do not plan a career as personal injury lawyers. At some schools virtually no one chooses to go into that line of work. Why, then, do all law schools require a course in Torts, something which has been true for at least the last one hundred years?

There are at least two reasons. Torts, of all the first year courses, is the one where most of the rule structure still comes from "common law"—that is to say, cases rather than statutes. While there are certainly statutes that are relevant in the study of Torts, there is no overarching codification like the Federal Rules of Civil Procedure, the Uniform Commercial Code, or the Model Penal Code. Learning how judges "make" law is crucial information for all lawyers. Your study of Torts enables you to see what kinds of judicial arguments are legitimate and what kinds are not, and to begin to get a sense of the appropriate sphere of responsibility of courts versus legislatures.

Second, Torts cases are very much fact driven. To study Torts is to become a fact junkie. Facts are, of course, important, in all areas of the law, but the precise details of how an accident came to pass are particularly crucial in deciding who should bear the expense of that accident. Many law students assume that in law school they will learn legal rules. By studying Torts you learn to appreciate the importance of facts. That, in turn, helps you become a better lawyer whether you choose to specialize in corporate law, intellectual property, labor law, or Bosnian Admiralty law.

4. Dealing With Being A One-L

A voluminous literature now exists on the psychic distress of law school. There is no doubt that first year in particular can sometimes be overwhelming and sometimes be demoralizing, and that is even before you begin brooding over issues like student loans and employment prospects.

Those who have studied happiness—yes, there really are such people—say that being happy is really the function of a relatively small number of factors. Among the most important: your sense of control; your degree of connectedness with others; working on tasks that are challenging without being overwhelming so that you have a sense of competence; and adopting a frame of reference that avoids constantly comparing yourself with unrealistic standards.[1]

Law school can tend to undermine all of these things.

- It deprives you of control—you must take courses that someone else has selected for you, you must answer questions without warning from professors, and you get little feedback on your work.

- Rather than promoting a sense of community, connectedness and common enterprise, law school seems to be the ultimate zero sum game where every other person in the building is a rival.

- The tasks you are asked to perform often leave you feeling incompetent, not because they are intrinsically difficult but because no one really explains what it is you are supposed to be doing and no one shows you how to do it.

- Finally, you are constantly being told about the most successful alumni from your school and the great judges and crusading lawyers from past history with the implicit suggestion that if you do not replicate their achievements you are a failure.

Little wonder law school makes people unhappy!

1 I am borrowing shamelessly here from Nancy Levit and Douglas O. Linder, *Happy Law Students, Happy Lawyers,* 58 Syracuse L. Rev. 351 (2008). The same authors have written an entire book on the subject called *The Happy Lawyer: Making A Good Life in the Law*. It would not be a bad use of your time to read either the article or the book.

As in medicine, however, a good diagnosis is the first step to a cure. You may not control your course selection or the classroom experience, but you control how you allocate your time, where you choose to study, what study aids you choose to use, and a host of other factors about your daily life. You have a lot more control than you think you do, and if you focus on the things you can control there is a good chance you will feel better about yourself and the experience of being a one-L.

While there are undeniably competitive aspects to law school, you can seek out like-minded classmates and build your own group of mutually supportive colleagues. Just as some areas of legal practice are competitive and some are collaborative, the same is true of cliques in law school. When you stop seeing everyone else as a scheming enemy, you will discover that you feel much more content with your life in law school.

You can cultivate a sense of competence by finding resources (perhaps even including this little book) that will clarify and demystify the material. Find a book with some multiple choice questions and use it for periodic review. You will quickly realize you have learned more than you think. Visit your professors during office hours—you will quickly get a sense of which ones are approachable. Conversations with them will convince you that you know what you are doing. Remembering that you are a capable and competent person is an important strategy in sustaining a positive mood.

Finally, you should make it a point to remember how fortunate you are. Try spending some of your time using your new legal skills to help those who are struggling to make it every day in our society. Just a few hours a month helping out at a local small claims court or Legal Aid office will wonderfully clarify your frame of reference. If you compare yourself with Oliver

Wendell Holmes, you may become dejected, but he's not in your section. Compared with most others in our society you are a gifted overachiever.

Of course, on any given day, law school can grind you down. It is also, however, an intellectual thrill ride. Just strap yourself in and enjoy—but be sure to keep your hands inside the car so you don't get hurt.

A Short & Happy Guide to Torts

CHAPTER I

The Intentional Torts

1. The Concept of Intent

It should not surprise you to learn that a plaintiff who alleges an intentional tort must prove that the defendant acted intentionally. That's why they are called intentional torts! The trick is that the concept of intent in the law is a bit more elaborate than the same concept in every day life.

A defendant acts intentionally when he has *either* of two states of mind. These two are entirely different from each other, and in a sense mutually exclusive. It is always helpful in cases like this to put labels on the concepts to keep them straight. So let us call the first state of mind—the first type of intent—"purpose" intent. A defendant has purpose-intent if he *desires* to bring about a legally forbidden consequence. It's not about doing some physical act "on purpose." Rather, it is about having a desire, a goal, an aim, an objective, a purpose (OK, enough synonyms) to accomplish something that the law forbids. The defendant has got to want it.

Now you cannot use this concept of intent, without knowing what the law forbids. In other words, it is *meaningless* without further knowledge concerning the specifics of the various intentional torts. So let's get slightly ahead of ourselves and take an example. There is a tort called False Imprisonment. The consequence that it forbids is "confinement"—with certain exceptions you can't confine someone against their will. Now let's say Dave* is a security guard at the law library. He is required to lock the door to all study rooms just before the building closes. As he passes room 16, he looks through the glass pane in the door and, seeing no one, he locks the door. However, the room is not empty. Pete,** a law student, is in the room and had been studying, but moments before Dave arrived on the scene, he decided to get down on the floor to practice one of his favorite yoga poses, which is why he wasn't visible through the window. When Pete finishes his yoga he discovers that he cannot get out of the room. He is confined.

So here's the question—if Dave the security guard is sued by Pete the student, will Pete be able to show that Dave acted intentionally? Under the definition we are working with the answer is no. Dave did not have the "purpose" to confine Pete, because he didn't even know Pete was there. True, he did lock the door "on purpose," but locking doors is not a legally forbidden consequence. It's all about the confinement, and Dave didn't want to confine anyone.

We said, however, that there are two kind of intent. We can call the second type of intent "knowledge intent." A person has this kind of intent if he acts knowing that a legally forbidden consequence is virtually certain to result, even if he doesn't want

* All potential **defendants** in this book have names that begin with a "**D**".

** All potential **plaintiffs** in this book have names that begin with a "**P**".

to produce that consequence. Now before we go any further, a little warning on verbiage. If you look this rule up in the Restatement of Torts, you will discover that it says the defendant must have knowledge to a "*substantial* degree of certainty." "Substantial" might sound to you like "pretty likely, but not guaranteed." That is an incorrect interpretation. The Restatement is written in a kind of stilted language. To the authors of that document, a "substantial degree of certainty" means something like 98% certain, as if you said "I'm substantially certain that Boise is the capital of Idaho," in the sort of pompous way that a law professor might say it. So don't let that formula throw you off. To have knowledge intent, the defendant must know that the forbidden consequence almost surely will come to pass.

Time for another example. Don is a native of Boston, transferred by his employer to a small town in rural Alabama. He hates it there. The slow pace of life, the hot sticky weather, and the absence of professional sports teams all make him miserable. One of the things he particularly hates is the monument to Confederate soldiers in the town square. It offends his Yankee sensibilities. So he puts together a bomb with a timer, plants it at the base of the monument, and sets it to go off the next day at noon. Don knows that many townspeople sit on the benches in the square to eat their lunch. Don knows that they are likely to be injured or killed by the bomb. However, it is not his *purpose* to injure or kill them. He is indifferent to them. He just wants to blow up the statue.

When Don's bomb explodes several persons are in fact badly injured. In due course, he is then sued for the tort called battery by one of those injured victims of the explosion. As we shall see shortly, the legally forbidden consequence involved in the battery tort is a "harmful or offensive bodily contact." Don certainly caused that—he harmed the body of the plaintiff—but plaintiff cannot recover unless Don acted intentionally. Given the facts, Don did not have the purpose to cause a harm to the body of the plaintiff—he was indifferent to the plaintiff and others like him—so there is no "purpose intent." However, he knew that this type of harm was virtually ("substantially") certain to happen. Given the placement of the bomb and his decision to set it to explode at noon, he had to know. So he has "knowledge intent" and can be held liable for the battery.

In the case law, a classic example of knowledge intent is *Garret v. Daily*. There, a five year old boy pulled a chair out from under an elderly woman who was about to sit down. She fell to the ground, was injured, and sued the kid for battery. Did he want to hurt her (did he have purpose-intent)? Who knows, who cares. The point is that he knew she would be hurt (knowledge intent). Even 5-year-olds understand the law of gravity, and since he knew she would fall, that is good enough in the eyes of the law. In the actual case, the trial court made the mistake of considering only purpose-intent, and the Supreme Court of Washington remanded to have them consider knowledge-intent.

There is still one further twist. Under the doctrine known as *transferred intent,* if a defendant desires to produce *any* consequence forbidden by the law with respect to *any* person (or if he knows that any such consequence is virtually certain to occur) the law says he has acted intentionally even if a *different* consequence occurs, or a *different* person is affected. Drew throws a rock at Polly wanting to hit her in the head, but his aim is off and he hits Paula instead. Paula sues for battery and Drew says, "I can't be liable because I lacked intent—I didn't mean to hit Paula. Nor did I have knowledge that she would be hit. I don't even know Paula. It was an accident." The court will reject this argument, because Drew had the necessary intent vis-a-vis Polly and that intent "transfers over" to the actual victim.

To be honest about it, the transferred intent rule is a legal fiction. In every day, common-sense terms, it really was an accident that Drew hit Paula with the rock. Saying that he did it intentionally or "on purpose" is a bit weird, or at least a bit lawyerly. However, characterizing situations like this as "intentional" permits the assessment of punitive damages, which seems justified because of the defendant's initial bad motivation. So we use a clumsy label to get to a desired result. This will not be the only time you will see that in the course of your legal education.

The notions of purpose-intent and knowledge-intent work pretty well with most ordinary folks. What happens, however, if the person being sued has reduced capacity? For instance, what if the person being sued is mentally ill, insane, or under the influence of drugs or alcohol or perhaps just a very young child? The answer is that we will ignore those facts, and treat the situation *as if the person had full legal capacity*. In other words, an insane person will be held liable for a battery if they punch you in the nose, a drunk will be held liable for false imprisonment if they lock you in a room, and a seven-year-old will be held liable for trespass if he comes into your yard without permission. Another way to put this rule is to say that there are no incapacity defenses in the field of intentional torts.

2. The Tort of Battery

A battery is usually defined as *the intentional infliction of a harmful or offensive bodily contact*. So a plaintiff must prove that the defendant (1) acted intentionally; (2) that he (the plaintiff) suffered either a harm, or offense; and (3) that the harm or offense involved a touch—a contact with the body. We have already considered intent, so let's look a bit more closely at the other two elements.

A defendant is only liable for battery if he inflicts a harmful or offensive bodily contact. A contact is harmful if it hurts. It makes the plaintiff bleed, breaks a bone, sends him to the hospital or makes him dead. The Restatement says a contact is harmful if it causes "physical impairment of the condition" of plaintiff's body, or if causes "physical pain or illness." It's not a hard concept. So when Dabney shoots Portnoy, or stabs him, or shoves him down a flight of stairs causing him to break both legs, the result is a harmful contact.

Offensiveness is bit more subtle. Some kinds of contacts are pretty much offensive to everyone. Perhaps a classic example is to spit in someone's face. The Restatement, with its oddly dated view of society, uses the example of flicking a glove in someone's face. No doubt offensive if you live in 18th-century France. For borderline cases, the test is whether the bodily contact in question would infringe or violate a "reasonable sense of personal dignity." In other words, to be offensive, the touching must be one that would be considered unacceptable by a normal person.

Consequently, routine touchings that people put up with as part of every day life are not offensive and are not batteries, even if they disturb the particular plaintiff involved in the incident. A tap on the shoulder to get someone's attention, or a gentle pat on the back to congratulate a co-worker on the birth of his son are thus not offensive as a matter of law whether or not they really, really bother the person who was touched. To put this more formally, the standard is an "objective" rather than a "subjective" one, meaning that the law does not take eccentricities into account.

Now what about the additional requirement, or element, that the harm or offense must involve a bodily contact? The most important point to bear in mind here is that the "body" in question is the body *of the plaintiff* or victim. The defendant does not have to use his own body to perpetrate the contact. In some cases, this is obvious. If I shoot you in the leg, I have inflicted a harmful contact on *your* body—namely the contact between the bullet and your leg—even though my body was not involved as it would be if I punched you. That one is easy because the contact happens instantaneously. The same result follows, however, even if there is a delay. For instance, say I sneak into your bedroom and put fire ants all over your bed sheets. Four hours later you lie down to take a nap and get some fierce ant bites. That would clearly be a battery as well. I caused a harmful contact to *your* body. While I didn't use my body, letting the ants do the dirty work, and while the contact didn't happen instantaneously, none of that matters.

One other small point deserves mention. The plaintiff's body is considered to include anything the plaintiff is holding or touching. Thus, if I snatch your purse as you are walking down the street, that is an offensive touching of your body even though I did not actually touch the skin of your hand. A famous case on this issue involved a bigoted hotel employee who snatched a plate from the hands of an African American patron about to serve himself at a buffet. That was a battery because the plate was considered part of the plaintiff's person. This rule is sometimes called the "extended personality" rule.

Of course all these rules—like all legal rules—become fuzzy at the boundaries. It is not always clear whether a given bodily contact offends a "reasonable" sense of dignity. If a teammate on your softball team gives you a pat on the rear end after you hit a home run, some might say that this is not a routine or acceptable touching because your rear end is an intimate part of your body, while others might say that it is acceptable because it is commonly done. Similarly, if someone deliberately blows cigarette smoke in your face to annoy you it is not clear if they have actually caused contact with your body. Smoke is not like a bullet, or even like the saliva of a spit in the face, but one could argue that it is composed of minute particles which qualify as sufficient to make a contact.

In the real world, such "boundary-questions" often require a court to make new law, and their resolution is unpredictable until a court finally rules on them. In law school, you will be expected to first, know that you are dealing with a boundary question on the edge of a definition, and second, to be able to make a persuasive argument for either result. There is no need to be flustered by these kinds of questions—once you see them for what they are, they are fun to argue about and they are why people actually need to hire lawyers.

3. The Tort of Assault

Battery is about the integrity of the body—that tort throws up a protective cocoon around your physical person and holds others liable if they deliberately invade it without your permission. Assault is about your peace of mind. However, it is a very narrow tort. It only protects you from one, very specific and narrowly defined, invasion of mental tranquility.

A defendant commits an assault if he intentionally puts the plaintiff in reasonable apprehension of an immediate battery. Distilled into elements, plaintiff must show (1) intent; (2) reasonable apprehension of battery; and (3) that the battery is imminent.

The first new element here is "apprehension" of a battery. While the word apprehension, in every day speech, may suggest fear, that is not required for the tort of assault. The defendant's conduct need not leave the plaintiff quaking in his boots, afraid for his safety or cowering in the corner. Remember, much of the terminology we are working with comes from case law and Restatement provisions that are decades old. Those sources use the word apprehension in an old fashioned (and pompous) way as a synonym for simple "knowledge." Back in the day, someone, especially a law professor or judge, might have said "I apprehend that the Dean will be making remarks this afternoon." While it's possible that the speaker might have been afraid of what the Dean would say, the meaning in this context is that *I know* or *I am aware* that the Dean will be speaking.

So, rendered in modern English, an assault plaintiff must prove that he *knew* that the defendant was about to touch him in a disagreeable way (that is, about to commit a battery). This means that if Dilbert raises his hand as if to strike Pomeroy in the *back of the head*, and then stops his gesture before making contact, Pomeroy could not recover for assault if he did not see it and did not know about it. On the other hand, if Dilbert made the same gesture as if he were going to slap Pomeroy in the cheek, Pomeroy would have a good claim, even if he were not afraid of Dilbert and quite confident in his ability to defend himself.

One brain teaser that can come up in this context is how to deal with the defendant who is bluffing. In this kind of case, the defendant makes what appears to be a threatening gesture, but lacks the ability to actually carry it to completion and commit an actual battery. The classic case would be pointing an unloaded gun at someone and threatening to fire. The gesture is menacing, but subsequent contact is impossible. If you remember that assault is about an intrusion on plaintiff's peace of mind, this case becomes fairly easy. We just need to figure out what the plaintiff knows.

If the plaintiff knows that the gun is unloaded, he knows he cannot be "touched" (that is, cannot be shot) and his mental tranquility is, in the eyes of the law, unaffected. Consequently, in such a case, the plaintiff cannot establish the tort of assault. If, however, the plaintiff does not know one way or the other whether the gun is loaded, it would be reasonable for him to assume that he might be shot. The tort only requires *reasonable* "apprehension," not *certain* apprehension, so that would be good enough to state a claim. The principle is somewhat more formally stated as: "apparent ability creates a reasonable apprehension." The key is to remember that you must focus on what is apparent *to the plaintiff.*

This takes us to the requirement of "imminence." Not every threatened battery is an assault. The prospective battery must be about to happen *right now.* In some cases, therefore, a defendant who makes a threatening gesture will escape assault liability because he says something that indicates that he does not propose to act immediately. For instance, assume Delilah approaches Petunia and, drawing her hand back as if to slap her says, "I would slap you silly if you weren't enrolled in Torts this semester." There is no assault here, because Delilah's statement makes it clear that she is not planning to touch Petunia *right this minute*. The same result would follow if she raised her arm as if to strike and said, "Just you wait until after Contracts this afternoon—that's when I will slap you silly." A threat of future harm—even when accompanied by a menacing gesture—is not an assault (though it may be some other tort, such as intentional infliction of emotional distress).

Some authorities note that a "mere verbal" threat cannot be an assault. This is because mere words are assumed to lack immediacy. Until the defendant engages in some kind of physical conduct or gesture, the notion is that "it's all talk." There aren't very many real world cases of this type because, in the real world, few people emulate motionless statues when delivering a threat. In any event, the "mere words" point is not really a sub-rule, but just a particular application of the requirement that the apprehension must relate to something that is about to happen immediately. It's not immediate until the defendant "makes a move."

4. The Tort of False Imprisonment

You can't just go around locking people up against their will. If you do that, you are liable for the tort of false imprisonment and will have to pay them damages to compensate them for the annoyance. The traditional elements of this tort are (1) intent; (2) an act of restraint; and (3) resulting confinement of the plaintiff within a bounded area.

An act of restraint can be a physical act, such as locking someone in a room. It can also be accomplished by taking an item of plaintiff's property, such as a purse containing plaintiff's keys and money, if the plaintiff would typically remain in the area in order to get the item back. It can also take the form of a threat, such as a claim that the plaintiff will be forcibly restrained or that a loved one will be harmed if he tries to leave the area. Of course, the threat must be plausible or realistic. Telling the plaintiff you will turn him into a unicorn if he leaves the room in the next half hour likely will not do it.

If the defendant has a pre-existing obligation to help the plaintiff move about, the failure to fulfill that obligation can itself be a form of restraint and can trigger liability for false imprisonment. For instance, assume Patrick agrees to take a boat trip with Devo, but makes Devo promise to take him ashore whenever he asks. When they arrive in New York harbor, there are no berths—no place for the boat to park. So Captain Devo drops anchor in the middle of New York Harbor. Patrick now asks to be taken ashore in a row boat, but Devo refuses. Devo is engaged in a form of restraint-by-omission, since he had an obligation to help Patrick get to his final destination ashore. This is essentially what happened in an old case called *Whittaker v. Sandford**.

Moral pressure is generally not considered sufficient duress to establish the tort of false imprisonment. Thus, in one case, an individual who had taken up residence with a religious sect was told that if she left, her family "would be damned in Hell forever." Some time later she was abducted by "deprogrammers" hired by her parents and, in due course, she sued the sect for false imprisonment. The court rejected the claim, chiefly because it felt that the statements of the sect members were protected under the First Amendment as religious speech.

Moreover, where the plaintiff opts to remain in a particular place voluntarily, there is, by definition, no restraint, and there is thus no false imprisonment. For instance, in some cases, when a plaintiff is accused of wrongdoing—often shoplifting—he or she might opt to remain in the store in order to prove his or her innocence. Determining whether the plaintiff has remained voluntarily, or as a result of duress, requires weighing the surrounding circumstances, such as the number of people who confronted the plaintiff, whether some of those were persons who had economic or legal power over the plaintiff (her boss, or a police officer), or what was said by those present during the encounter. All such facts are fair game and it is ultimately up to the jury to decide if there was impermissible coercion.

---

* 110 Me. 77, 85 A. 399 (1912).

If the plaintiff is unaware of the confinement, there can be no recovery unless the plaintiff suffered some sort of physical harm. Thus, if I lock you in your bedroom while you are sound asleep and then unlock the door an hour later, you have no cause for complaint unless you woke up and tried to exit the room. By way of contrast, if a nurse locks an unconscious diabetic patient in an exam room for an hour and the patient suffers organ damage because he was denied treatment during that period, the patient would clearly be entitled to recover despite having had no consciousness that he had been confined.

Which takes us to the final requirement—that the confinement be in a "bounded area." This means that not every interference with free movement counts as false imprisonment. Blocking the plaintiff's movements in only one direction would not constitute false imprisonment. Excluding plaintiff from a place of business or denying him entry to a public facility is also not actionable false imprisonment (though it may violate some other law, like a statute). Thus, when the bouncer at the hottest club in town refuses to let you in because you are insufficiently "cool," you will not be able to pursue a false imprisonment claim against either him or the club.

In some cases, the area in which the plaintiff is confined is not entirely bounded—there is a way out. If that way out would be dangerous or humiliating or otherwise impractical, however, the law treats the situation as equivalent to confinement in a bounded area. The test is whether the possible exit is a reasonable means of escape.

Assume that Darwin locks Pascal in a basement, but that Pascal could exit by crawling through a window. If the window is relatively easy to access, and relatively large, and it would not require much physical effort to leave via that window, Pascal is not really imprisoned, and Darwin is not liable for false imprisonment. On the other hand, if the window is small, or high up on the wall and difficult to reach, or would require Pascal to deal with shards of broken glass, it would not be a reasonable exit; Pascal is effectively imprisoned and Darwin is liable, even though the area is not hermetically sealed up. No one can force you to get shredded on broken glass in order to proceed on your merry way. That's just not right.

5. The Tort of Intentional Infliction of Emotional Distress

Intentional infliction of emotional distress is a rather modern tort, first arriving on the legal scene only in the middle of the last century. It is sometimes called intentional infliction of *mental* distress, and sometimes just called "outrage." We will call it IIED for the sake of brevity. In order to establish this tort plaintiff must show (1) defendant acted either intentionally or recklessly; (2) defendant engaged in extreme and outrageous conduct; and (3) as a result, plaintiff suffered severe distress.

Note that, unlike the other intentional torts, a defendant can be held liable for IIED even though he did not act intentionally, if the plaintiff can show that defendant was "reckless." Recklessness means that the defendant acted in utter disregard of the plaintiff's emotional well-being.

In determining whether the defendant's conduct is "extreme and outrageous" courts ask, in the first instance, whether the conduct in question exceeds all bounds of decency tolerated in a civilized society. In most cases this will be a question for the jury—they are the ones who get to decide if the behavior was simply boorish and ill-mannered or if it went so far beyond the pale as to deserve legal condemnation. The problem is that this "bounds of decency" rule is very vague and highly subjective. The little old lady who sings in the church choir may have a very different view of where the line of decency lies than her 23-year-old hard-drinking, mohawk-sporting grandson who works as the manager of a local strip club.

Appellate courts have tried to provide some consistency in this area by identifying certain patterns of conduct that tend to make a finding of outrageousness more appropriate. Bear in mind that conduct that does not fit within one of these patterns can still be found outrageous. That said, a large number of cases decided for plaintiffs do fit within one or more of the following scenarios.

First, courts consider whether the defendant's conduct was continuous or on-going. An isolated incident might not be outrageous, but that same incident repeated over and over again can become intolerable. Consider the crude co-worker who makes a vulgar sexual proposition to someone else in the office. Inappropriate? Sure. Distressing? Probably. A tort? Doubtful. However, if that person keeps making those kinds of remarks to the same colleague at work over a period of weeks, the conduct is much more likely to be characterized as outrageous.

Another common pattern involves abuse of authority. If the defendant is your supervisor at work, a particular course of conduct might be more outrageous and more distressing than if he were merely a co-worker. Go back to that last example. If your boss makes the crude and inappropriate sexual overture you probably have an immediate sense that this is particularly unacceptable and you might be far more agitated by the episode than if it was merely a colleague who acted in this fashion. A similar analysis might apply if a landlord vindictively refuses to provide basic services to a tenant, if a creditor threatens financial ruin when a debtor is only a few days late with a payment, or if a police officer or other governmental official is abusive to a member of the public who is already in distress, such as a crime victim.

Bear in mind, however, that in the employment context, some courts have stressed that supervisors at work must have latitude to discipline employees, and those courts have expressed reluctance to micro-manage the workplace. So the fact that a partner at a law firm screams at you and tells you that your memo is "crap" is not likely, absent more, to be outrageous.

Yet another common scenario in the IIED cases involves a defendant who targets a plaintiff who is emotionally vulnerable, or who engages in conduct designed to exploit the plaintiff's particular sensitivities. For instance, if Daedalus knows that Pandora is particularly fond of her pet armadillo, and if, in order to distress her, he deliberately drops a brick on the creature in her presence, there is a good chance that this behavior would be found outrageous. This is what we might call deliberately "pressing someone's buttons."

Sometimes a defendant will direct his conduct at one person in a way that distresses someone else. To take an extreme case, a defendant might shoot Alan, and Betty might be very distressed by that conduct because she knows Alan, or because she observes the shooting and finds it horrific. In these cases, the direct victim of the shooting (Alan) will, of course, have a remedy for battery (if that person is dead, this cause of action can be pursued by his or her estate). The other party—Betty—can persuasively argue that shooting Alan was "outrageous." She can also argue that even if the shooter did not have a purpose of distressing her, he should have known to a virtual certainty that such distress would result, and this is enough to establish "knowledge" intent. Even if no intent can be shown, the shooter was certainly recklessly indifferent to Betty's emotions. Nonetheless, recovery will not be automatic for Betty. She must overcome two more hurdles.

First, Betty must have been present to observe the conduct directed at Alan—she must have been there when he was shot and seen it as it happened. If Betty did not learn that Alan had been shot until some time after the fact, she will not be allowed to recover, no matter how distressed she was. In addition, there must be a "plus factor." That can be either that the observer (Betty in our example) and the direct victim (Alan) are family members *or* that the observer suffered physical consequences from the distress. Thus, if Betty is Alan's wife or daughter, she would satisfy this second requirement. Alternatively, if Betty is Alan's roommate and she had a heart attack upon seeing him shot, she would also satisfy this second requirement.

These requirements are supposedly designed to keep the scope of liability for a single act to reasonable proportions. Without these rules, the bank robber who shoots a pedestrian on a crowded street while fleeing from the bank could be liable to dozens of distressed bystanders, and thousands more who learn about the events on the evening news, because his act is outrageous, and because he knows to a virtual certainty that many of those who learn about, let alone witness, a cold-blooded murder will be distressed. Whether we really should be worried about imposing excessive tort liability on murderous bank robbers is a question you can mull on your own, but the fear that a single act could trigger valid tort claims by thousands of plaintiffs is the traditional justification for these somewhat artificial limiting principles.

Recall that there is one more element for the tort of intentional infliction of emotional distress. It is not enough for recovery that the defendant engaged in outrageous conduct. The plaintiff must also suffer "severe distress." This requirement is indeterminate—there is no bright line test to give the verbal formula precise content. Some courts say that the distress must be so severe that no reasonable person should be expect to endure it, but frankly, that doesn't help much. Beyond that, courts do not usually demand any particular type of evidence or proof—there are no bright line tests. Thus, it is not *required* that the plaintiff sought medical attention for the distress; nor is plaintiff *required* to prove that the distress resulted in physical symptoms (like a heart attack); nor is it *required* that the plaintiff prove that he or she missed any particular number of days of work. The plaintiff can simply testify under oath that he was very distressed, and if the jury believes him, that would be sufficient.

Bear in mind, however, that in the real world, plaintiffs are cross-examined. If, on cross, they admit that they never saw a doctor, never missed a day of work and had no other symptoms of consequence, there is a good chance the jury may be skeptical of their claim of distress and deny recovery, or perhaps even that the judge will direct a verdict against them.

6. The Tort of Trespass to Land

As you will learn when you study the law of property, one of the key attributes of ownership is a right of "exclusive possession." That means, among other things, that if you own a piece of real estate, such as a farm, a vacant lot, or a house in the suburbs, no one can enter the property without your permission. If someone does enter without permission, they are liable for the tort of trespass.

The traditional elements of this tort are (1) intent, (2) possession of the property by the plaintiff and (3) and act of physical invasion of the property by the defendant. It is not necessary for a plaintiff to be the *owner* of the property in order to sue for the tort of trespass. Rather, it is only required that you have a present right of possession. In plain English, this means that if you are a tenant, merely renting a house or apartment for the semester, and someone comes into the house or apartment without your permission, you are the one with a claim for trespass. Indeed, your landlord would only have a claim if the trespasser does some sort of damage that imposes costs on the landlord—such as by damaging the plumbing in ways that require the landlord to spend money on repairs.

The required act of physical invasion can take place in either of two alternative fashions. First, the defendant can enter the property, on foot or in some kind of vehicle such as a car or boat. In such a case, the defendant need not know that he crossed a boundary line. In other words, a mistake about entitlement to enter the property is no defense. Assume that Delilah is hiking in a state park and after meandering down a trail for an hour, she leaves the park property and enters land own by Paula. Delilah is liable for trespass on these facts. If she protests that she did not act intentionally, the answer is that she did have the purpose of getting to the location where she wound up—she deliberately put one foot in front of the other and walked there—and that is all that is required for liability.

If you are concerned about poor Delilah in this situation, bear in mind that she could have taken steps to familiarize herself with the location of the boundary lines of the park in advance. In effect, the rule that makes her liable is a rule that suggests that she really ought to buy a map. Moreover, bear in mind that in a case such as this, Delilah's trespass is purely "technical." Since she did not do any actual harm to Paula's property, she will be liable only for "nominal" damages, usually assessed as one dollar. That means, in turn, that in the real world, Paula would not be likely to bother with a lawsuit since it would be difficult to find a lawyer who would take a case where the traditional one-third contingency fee would amount to 33 cents.

The second way that a defendant can commit the impermissible act of physical invasion necessary for the tort of trespass is by throwing or propelling a tangible object onto the plaintiff's property. An obvious example arises when Darius deliberately throws a rock through his neighbor Pamela's window—although Darius did not himself enter her property, he is liable for trespass for this invasion and Pamela can recover the cost of repairing the window.

Bear in mind, however, that we are still dealing with an intentional tort. If Darius had been playing catch with his son and carelessly threw the ball so that it smashed Pamela's window, Darius would be liable for negligence, not for trespass. On the other hand, if Desmond, an ardent member of the NRA, erroneously thought he owned a small shed located 100 yards behind his house and decided to shoot out several of the windows with his rifle, just for target practice, he would be liable for a trespass if it turned out that someone else owned the shed. He deliberately propelled the tangible object (the bullet) onto someone else's property, and his mistake about the ownership of the property is similar to hiking-Delilah's mistake about the boundary of the state park earlier in this section. Clumsy or uncoordinated people are not trespassers; stupid and ill-informed people can be.

Under the traditional rule, propelling *intangible* items onto someone else's land is not treated as a trespass, no matter how unpleasant the consequences. Torturing your neighbor by playing your radio at a loud, obnoxious volume at all hours of the day and night, or shining bright lights through his window so that he cannot sleep, does not interfere with his exclusive right of physical possession of the property, only with his rights to use and enjoy the property. Such behavior can be remedied, if at all, through the cause of action for "nuisance," which we will look at towards the end of this short and happy tour of tort law.

One who originally entered another's property with permission—or who permissibly stored his stuff on someone else's land—can become a trespasser if he refuses to leave (or remove his stuff) after the permission expires. Thus, if you refuse to leave your friend's home at the end of a dinner party you can be held liable for trespass even though you were invited to enter at the start of the evening. Same result if you refuse to leave a retail store at closing time after being asked to do so. Ditto if you refuse to take your car off of a parking lot or out of a garage after your pre-paid period of parking has expired.

Although most trespass situations involve a defendant entering onto—or throwing something onto—the surface of the plaintiff's property, the plaintiff can also recover for entries above or below the surface, provided they are at a reasonable distance from the ground. Thus it is trespass to (deliberately) throw a ball (or fire a bullet) over your neighbor's back yard, even if the ball (or bullet) never touches the ground, and lands on the far side of his yard in the public street. The same rule follows if you extend a branch of your coal mine under an adjacent parcel of land. The qualification that the distance must be reasonable avoids the preposterous result of imposing liability for such things as ordinary aircraft flights that routinely pass far above private lands, or for the construction of subway tunnels that might pass under them but at a very significant depth.

It is also not generally considered a trespass if trees, or tree roots on one person's land extend or project into the neighbor's air space or under the surface of his land. If those projecting limbs or roots do some actual harm, the victimized neighbor might have a claim for nuisance, but the simple invasion of the air or soil is not considered a sufficient violation of possession to warrant a trespass remedy. Moreover, the neighbor is usually allowed to lop off the intruding limbs if he likes.

7. Torts Violating Interests in Personal Property

Personal property is the legal label for everything you own other than real estate. In some legal systems, these are called "moveables" or "personalty" (in contrast to realty), and a somewhat older legal term for such items was "chattels." Examples of personal property include your car, truck or boat, your hat, gloves or coat, your expensive watch, and your bottle of scotch, your nice fluffy bed, or your spool of red thread, your cute dog or cat and your straw welcome mat.[1] There is a modern trend to treat various intangible items of value, such as computer files, customer lists, or cable TV signals as items of personal property as well.

It is a tort to intentionally "interfere" with someone else's personal property. One can interfere with your property by deliberately damaging it in some way. Alternatively, they could interfere with your property by using it without your permission or taking it away from you, either temporarily or permanently (which would, of course, be theft). If the degree of interference is relatively slight, the appropriate cause of action is known as

1 Apologies to Dr. Seuss.

trespass to chattels. Thus, if someone takes your pen home, keeps it overnight, and returns it the next day, or if someone deliberately pulls a button off your coat, you will have a cause of action for trespass to chattels.

By contrast, when the degree of interference becomes significant, the plaintiff has the option of suing for the tort known as *conversion*. This would be the case if someone stole your car, or if someone hurled your laptop against a brick wall, smashing it to smithereens. In a conversion case, the plaintiff is entitled to recover the full market value of the item involved, not just the costs of rental or repair. For instance, if the damage to your laptop could be repaired for $600, but it was brand new and you had recently purchased it for $1500, you could recover the full $1500 in your suit for conversion. If it was one year old and the fair market value of a one year old laptop of that make and model was $900, that would be your amount of recovery. For this reason, it is sometimes said that conversion operates as a "forced sale." The defendant who substantially interferes with your personal property is effectively obligated to buy it from you.

Under the traditional common law rule, an innocent purchaser from a converter is also liable for the tort of conversion. If John steals Pierre's watch, and then sells it to Dominic, Pierre will have a valid claim for conversion against Dominic, who either must either return the watch to Pierre or pay him for it. The Uniform Commercial Code (in § 2-403) does recognize an exception to this rule. When an owner of a chattel entrusts it to a merchant who deals in goods of that kind, one who buys the item from that merchant will not be a converter even if the merchant sold it without authorization. Thus, if you bring your laptop to a computer store for repairs, and they sell it to an unknowing customer, you will have a conversion claim against the store, but not against the customer.

As with the tort of trespass to land, a mistake about ownership of the item in question, or about entitlement to use or possess it, is no defense. In other words, if you take my cell phone thinking that it is yours, and keep it overnight, I will have a valid claim of trespass to chattels against you, notwithstanding your innocent error. It is enough to show intent that you took the phone on purpose. The fact that everyone in the world has the exact same iPhone will not preclude liability. Of course, if you *accidentally* knock the phone off a table and thereby damage it, you would be liable, if at all, only for negligence.

CHAPTER 2

Defenses to Intentional Torts

1. Consent

If you give someone permission to invade your interests, you cannot turn around and complain about it in a court of law after the fact. This is the basic idea of consent. It operates as a defense to all of the intentional torts.

The first point to bear in mind is that only a person with legal "capacity" can consent. It follows that those who have a mental infirmity—such as those who are mentally ill or under the influence of drugs or alcohol—cannot give a valid consent. This makes intuitive sense. If you ask someone tripping on LSD if you can punch him in the nose and he says, "sure thing dude, sounds groovy," this is not the kind of thoughtful permission the law is looking for. When you punch him you will be liable for battery and, if you argue consent, you will be laughed out of court.

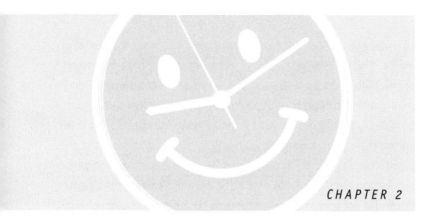

Children pose an interesting case. They lack the maturity, judgment and experience of adults, but, to the surprise of some parents, the law does not consider them to be entirely mentally infirm. Thus, children can consent to age-appropriate invasions of their interests. Two 12-year-old boys can agree to wrestle and their consent to wrestle will preclude either from suing the other for battery for the offensive or harmful touchings that take place during their bout. On the other hand, a 12-year-old cannot consent to surgery. A similar rule would likely apply to someone with a moderate developmental disability. That person can consent to things he is capable of understanding, but not to invasions that are beyond his comprehension.

Assuming plaintiff has legal capacity, the easiest type of consent fact pattern involves an "express" consent. This is an explicit statement by the plaintiff giving the defendant permission to act in a way that would otherwise be an intentional tort. When guests come to your home and you say, "oh, hi, come on in," you have given them express consent. That is why, logically enough, you can't turn around and sue them for trespassing in your house. Similarly, when you go to the barber and say, "take a little off the top," you have given him express consent to cut your hair, and he won't be liable for battery when he starts snipping away.

However, an express consent will not bar an intentional tort claim if the defendant obtained that consent through fraud or duress. Duress is force or coercion. Assume that Daniel accosts Parnell in a dark alley and, drawing a gun, says, "give me your wallet." As Parnell begins to hand over the wallet Daniel remembers the consent rule from torts and says, "wait a minute—before you give me your wallet I want you to say 'I consent to you taking my wallet and keeping it as gift.' Come on, say it or I shoot." So Parnell, extremely frightened by this legally sophisticated mugger, says the phrase, whereupon Daniel takes the wallet and flees. When Daniel is eventually arrested, Parnell sues him for conversion of the wallet. At the trial of that claim Daniel says, "it can't be conversion because he gave me express consent to take his wallet," and quotes the words he made Parnell utter. That is, of course, ridiculous. Having obtained the consent under duress, Daniel cannot rely on it to excuse his own subsequent conduct.

The fraud principle is pretty similar. In this variation, the defendant tells a lie or keeps key information secret in order to induce the plaintiff to give consent. For instance, the imposter who dresses up as a doctor and secures consent to touch intimate parts of the plaintiff's body on the pretext that the touchings are medically necessary will be liable for a battery. A claim of "consent" in such a case will fail because the defendant obtained the consent through fraud.

Consent, however, need not be "express" or "explicit." It can be implied. This is where things get a little more interesting. One common situation arises when the plaintiff engages in an activity or goes to a place where certain tortious invasions are customary or routine. The law assumes that the plaintiff is aware of the custom and thus has consented to the invasions. Thus, when you play football with your friends, you "consent" to getting tackled. If you sued an opposing player for battery not only would your friends think you were really weird and refuse to ever play with you again, but you would lose your lawsuit, because you impliedly consented to being tackled when you opted to play. Similarly, when you go to the doctor's office you consent to being touched in the various ways that are customary during a medical exam even if you never utter the words "you may touch me" out loud.

Implied consent can also arise from the circumstances surrounding an encounter between two people. We are all entitled to "read the situation" and make reasonable interpretations about what behavior is permissible based on the objective conduct of others. Consider the typical romantic evening. Two individuals are seated next to each other on the sofa, sipping wine and chatting amiably. There is a lull in the conversation and one leans over and gives the other a kiss. Battery? Probably not. If a reasonable person would have concluded, based on body language, the earlier events of the evening, and all the other surrounding circumstances that a kiss was welcome, there is an implied consent to engage in that behavior.

One early case illustrating this idea is *O'Brien v. Cunard Lines*. O'Brien was a young lady, aged 17, emigrating to the United States from Ireland. En route, passengers were told that they needed smallpox vaccinations in order to be admitted to the U.S. They were invited to line up and get those vaccinations onboard the ship. When O'Brien reached the front of that line, she told the doctor she had already been vaccinated back home. The doctor responded that she did not have the scar or "mark" on her arm that was a characteristic of a smallpox vaccination. At that point, O'Brien said and did nothing further. She did not walk away, she did not cover her shoulder, she did not roll down the sleeve of her blouse. The doctor then vaccinated her. When she sued for a battery, the court found that there was "implied consent." The doctor "read the situation" and reasonably concluded that she was willing to get the vaccine, and the court thus denied her relief.

A consent once given—whether express or implied—does not endure eternally. It can be revoked. Having agreed to play football, you can quit the game after the first half. If another player tackles you as you walk to your car, you will have a good claim of battery against that player, because your earlier (presumably implied) consent to batteries associated with the play of the game ended when you stopped playing. Of course, a revocation of consent must be given under circumstances where the other party can reasonably respond to it. If you visit an amusement park and get on the roller coaster, you impliedly consent to being "imprisoned" for the duration of the ride. If, as the coaster approaches the first big drop you scream, "I revoke my consent! Let me the hell out of hereeeeeee!"—that revocation will not be valid.

In addition, all consent has a scope. If another party exceeds the scope of the consent given, that other party will be liable for a tort. When you go shopping you have an implied consent from the shop-keeper to enter the premises. That is "consent by operation of custom." However, the scope of the consent is limited. You are not allowed to enter the back storeroom of the premises, or the manager's office, and if you do, you have exceeded the scope of consent and will be liable for trespass. When a patient explicitly consents to a surgical procedure on his toe, the doctor is not permitted to operate on the patient's ear, and if she does, it is beyond the scope of consent, and hence a battery. Of course, it is not always clear just what precise "scope" of consent plaintiff intended. A good lawyer is one who can use the facts to make a persuasive argument on that issue.

2. Self-Defense, Defense of Others, and Defense of Property

The law does not expect you to stand idly by if someone is about to punch you in the nose, or for that matter, about to rob your laptop. You are allowed to respond reasonably—even in a way that would otherwise be a tort—and because you are responding to a threat, your conduct is immunized from tort liability. In other words, if you punch an assailant to prevent him from punching you, you will not be liable for a battery. We can call the legal rules that capture this idea the "protective privileges." There are three principle defenses in this category—self-defense, defense of others, and defense of property.

In order for a defendant to invoke a protective privilege, his or her alleged tortious behavior must occur in response to an *imminent* threat. In other words, the defendant must act "in the heat of the moment." If someone raises their hand to strike you, you have a legal privilege to grab their hand or push them away—you will not be liable for a battery. Once the threat has passed, however, there is no longer any privilege. If someone hits you, you cannot wait three days, then go to their house and punch them in the nose. That would not be self-defense, it would be revenge, and the protective privileges do not encompass revenge. You must strike while the iron is hot, or else you will be liable for a tort.

In addition, the party invoking a protective privilege must have a reasonable belief that the threat is imminent. This means that a mistake about the situation will not necessarily deprive one of the privilege, if the mistake was a reasonable one. If Portnoy, while standing close to Dirk, rapidly raises his hand to smooth out his hair, but a reasonable person would think that Portnoy was preparing to strike a blow, Dirk would be privileged to grab Portnoy's arm. Obviously, in cases like this, everything depends on the facts, and the parties will likely differ about whether or not Dirk acted reasonably. That's why we have lawyers and juries.

Even when a party is privileged to act defensively, his or her response must be limited to the force necessary under the circumstances. The use of excessive force destroys the privilege and renders the user liable for a tort. Thus, if someone is about to slap you, you can grab their arm, but it would be a bit much for you to pull out a gun and shoot them, so if you opt to do that, you can expect to be held liable for a battery. In cases involving life-threatening situations, this rule means that one can respond with deadly force. Deadly force would not be appropriate however for lesser physical threats, and it is never an appropriate response to a threat against your property—you do not have a privilege to shoot someone who is running off with your cell phone. It follows that you also cannot use deadly mechanical devices to protect property, such as a shotgun trap to protect an unoccupied building, as the court held in the celebrated case of *Katko v. Briney*.[1]

There are a few more rules about the protective privileges worth noting. First, courts have traditionally held that a party entitled to use self-defense has no duty to retreat. Even if one can avoid injury by fleeing the scene, there is a right to "stand one's ground" and resort to self-defense without fear of tort liability. This "no retreat" rule does not apply, however, to cases involving deadly force unless the defendant is in his own home. If someone pulls out a knife during a law school mixer and threatens to stab you for speaking too often in Torts class, you must run away if you can safely do so. If, instead, you shoot the dude with the knife you will be liable for battery.

Second, in cases involving threats to property, one must first request the other "to desist" or reasonably believe that such a request would be useless. So if you return home from work to find someone having a picnic on your front lawn, you must first ask them to leave. Only after they refuse may you resort to reasonable force to expel them.

Finally, the privileges do not permit a party to inflict injury on an innocent bystander. In other words, if Jason is about to shoot Jessica, Jessica does not have a privilege to grab Sarah

1 183 N. W. 2d 657, 1971.

and use her as a human shield. If Jessica does that, she would be liable to Sarah. The Restatement (Second) of Torts has a delightful example along somewhat similar lines:

> *A, while driving B, a child of three, in a sleigh, is pursued by a pack of wolves which are rapidly closing upon him. To gain time A throws B to the wolves. The time consumed by the wolves in devouring B enables A to reach shelter a few seconds before the pack can reach him. A is subject to liability under a wrongful death statute for the death of B.*[2]

Lovely. Note, however, that if a person *accidentally* injures an innocent party in course of engaging in legitimate and reasonable self-defense against an aggressor, there would be no liability to that innocent party.

3. Public and Private Necessity

The necessity defenses permit an individual confronted with a sudden emergency to engage in certain acts that would otherwise be considered torts against property. In other words, to deal with the emergency a person may be allowed to trespass on someone else's real estate, or to take, use, or even destroy someone else's personal property (such as their car, or a supply of food or fuel) with either reduced tort liability or no liability at all. In the "real world" the necessity defenses are not raised very often. Nonetheless, they are theoretically interesting and law professors love them, so they are worth knowing a bit about.

---

2 This is not, strictly speaking, a self-defense situation because the wolves are not human aggressors.

There are actually two different necessity doctrines. The first is *public* necessity. This doctrine provides a complete defense for a person who commits a property tort to avert an imminent public disaster.

The facts of one leading public necessity case—*Surrocco v. Geary*—involved a fire raging in San Francisco on Christmas Eve in 1849. At that time all the houses in the town were, of course, relatively primitive wood structures, and the fire was rapidly moving from one to the next, threatening to destroy the entire city. Geary thought he could mitigate the disaster by creating a "fire break"—a gap in the row of houses where the fire would run out of adjacent fuel and thus stop spreading. So he ran to Surrocco's house and blew it up. Surrocco was not pleased.

You may think that Surrocco had little to complain about, as his house would have been destroyed when the fire reached it in any event. However, when Geary destroyed it, Surrocco was trying to move his belongings out onto a cart, and thus, Geary's intervention resulted in the loss of that property as well.[3] In any event, Surrocco sued Geary for destroying his property (the torts alleged today would be trespass, with regard to the house, and conversion with regard to the personal goods). The California Supreme Court invoked the public necessity doctrine, however, and determined that Geary should not be liable.

The logic of the public necessity doctrine is pretty obvious. In the middle of an emergency, we do not want potential good samaritans hesitating, in a Hamlet-like bout of indecision,

3 Geary, as it turns out, was the mayor, but the opinion makes it clear that he was being sued in his "private capacity" as an individual citizen. If you are from San Francisco or visit that lovely city you will find a Geary Street running the full width of the peninsula from the Bay to the Pacific.

because of fear of legal liability. By giving them an immunity to act free from the risk of legal liability we hope and expect that they will do so, and avert great harm, even if some individual must bear a loss as a consequence.

The *private* necessity doctrine involves a slight tweak of the basic fact pattern, with a significant change in the resulting legal treatment. In these cases, a person confronts an emergency that poses a threat only to his or her own interests. The impending disaster, in other words, threatens the (soon-to-be) defendant's property, or physical safety but does not otherwise impose a risk of harm on the public at large. For instance, a person might be stuck out of doors in a terrible snow-storm, or at sea during a gale, with risk to his own life and limb. Or a person's valuable farm animals might be threatened by some hazard such as attacking predators that do not threaten others. What should the law do if the threatened person grabs someone else's property or trespasses on someone else's land in a case such as this?

The general response to private necessity has been something of a compromise. The person making unconsented use of another's property is usually obligated to pay for any harm he causes to that property. If a person breaks down the door of a shed to take shelter during a blizzard, he will have to pay the owner of the shed to repair the door. If he uses someone else's gun to kill the wolves threatening his livestock, he will have to pay for the bullets he used and a fair rental fee for the time he had the gun. In legal terms, one remains liable to pay *compensatory* damages for a property tort in a private necessity situation.

However, if there is no harm done to the plaintiff's property—in other words if the invasion is only a "nominal" or "technical" one—there will be no liability. If you take shelter in a shed with an open door during a blizzard, you will not be held liable for the trespass even though you entered the land without permission. If you were sued, the property owner could not recover the traditional "one dollar" in nominal damages, nor could he recover punitive damages to "teach you a lesson." Your technical or nominal tort is excused in light of the emergency.

Moreover, whether or not harm has been committed to property, the property owner cannot throw the other party off his land as long as the emergency continues. Normally, of course, you can demand that a trespasser leave your property and if he does not do so you may then resort to reasonable, non-lethal force to get him to depart. This rule, however, is suspended in cases of emergency. Consequently, the property owner must tolerate the other person's presence, like it or not, until it is safe for that other person to be on his way. To put the same point the other way around, a person has an affirmative right to enter someone else's real estate without permission in an emergency to protect their own safety or the safety of their goods.

A celebrated case called *Ploof v. Putnam* illustrates this last point. The Ploof family was sailing on Lake Champlain in a sailing vessel known as a sloop. Yes, they were in Ploof's sloop, which you really should try saying rapidly three or more times in a row. In any event, a severe storm arose and they decided to take refuge by tying their boat up to the dock on a private island owned by Mr. Putnam. Putnam was apparently not a nice fellow. He instructed his servant to untie their boat, and the docile servant obediently complied. The result was damage to the sloop and injuries to the Ploofs. The Ploofs sued for what we would now call trespass to chattels and conversion. The Supreme Court of Vermont found in their favor, concluding that the nature of the emergency justified their entry on the land, and that Putnam had no right to expel them while the storm was raging.

The private necessity rules have captured the imagination of those disposed to an economic analysis of tort law. They point out that by forcing a person faced with an emergency to pay for any actual damage he causes to someone else's property, the rules encourage such a person to take the least costly course of action. If his own goods are highly valuable and can be saved by doing only minor damage to the property of someone else, a rational person will save his valuable goods and pay the other party damages. But if one's own goods are only modestly valuable, and can only be saved by doing extensive harm to someone else's property, the rule requiring payment deters the owner of the goods from inflicting the wasteful harm to the other person's property. In econ-speak this is known as forcing the actor to "internalize an externality." There is more to the economic analysis of this situation, of course, but going into it is no way to keep a book either short or happy.

4. More Obscure Defenses

There are a number of other defenses that the law recognizes in specific situations. Most of these are relatively narrow in scope, or have faded in importance in recent decades. Let us take a very brief look at a few of these to conclude this chapter.

Most jurisdictions recognize a "discipline" privilege. This allows parents to engage in reasonable acts of discipline of their children, such as spanking them or confining them to their room, without being liable for battery or false imprisonment, as the case may be. The privilege is lost if the parent exceeds reasonable bounds, and indeed, unreasonable physical abuse of children is also a crime in every jurisdiction. In many states this rule also extends to those who stand in the shoes of parents, or as we say in Latin, those who are *in loco paren-*

tis. Examples would include teachers, camp counselors, or baby sitters. Of course, what is reasonable for a parent might be unreasonable for a teacher. Moreover, in many states teachers are forbidden by law or regulation from touching a student in any fashion.

The defenses of "reentry on land" and "recapture of chattels" are largely self-explanatory, and increasingly obsolete. The first of these rules allowed a person entitled to immediate possession of land to commit torts such as battery in the process of retaking the land from someone who had wrongfully and forcibly dispossessed him. Where this defense is available, one must first make a demand that the usurper vacate the premises before resorting to force. However, many states have passed "forcible entry" statutes that make it a crime to engage in such acts as breaking down doors in order to regain possession, and quite a few states even grant the wrongful possessor a civil remedy against the owner who regains possession through the use of force. Similarly, the recapture of chattels privilege allowed an owner to use force (without fear of tort liability) to recover an item of personal property that had been wrongfully taken from him.

These are, of course, forms of "self-help." The owner of the property could, of course, sue the person who had unjustifiably taken up residence in his house or who had stolen his car or laptop instead of physically confronting him, and the modern hostility to these two privileges suggests a preference for legal rather than physical resolution of disputes over property.

Note that while these two privileges resemble the general "defense of property" concept we have studied above, there is a timing difference. To invoke defense of property, you must generally act when the threat to your property is imminent or under way, but while you still have possession. With the two doctrines just mentioned, the lawful owner has already lost possession and is acting after-the-fact.

There are many additional privileges that allow entry on land without permission in special cases. For instance, a traveler on a public highway who reasonably believes that the road is impassible has a privilege to enter adjacent land in order to continue on his way. Persons may also be privileged to enter property to serve civil court papers or to effectuate an arrest for a crime. A passenger on a public train or bus has a privilege to use chattels "necessary to the enjoyment of the facility." So, you'll be glad to know that it's not a trespass to chattels for you to use the headphones in the seat back pocket in front of you without asking the airline for permission first.

Negligence: An Introduction and the Concept of Duty

1. An Introduction to Negligence

It is a sad reality that whenever we act there is some chance that we may inadvertently hurt someone (or someone's property) as a byproduct of our action. How much of a chance will depend on *how* we act—carefully or carelessly—but the only way to insure that there is a *zero* chance of injury would be to refrain from all action entirely. While lying completely inert in bed under the covers does have a certain appeal, most of us would find that boring after a while. So inevitably, as we go about our daily affairs, some folks will get hurt.

The law of negligence is essentially a system for trying, prospectively, to reduce the number of these accidental injuries to manageable or "appropriate" levels while, at the same time, retroactively compensating those who do get hurt if—but only if—the harm could have been avoided fairly easily. This means that negligence law does not provide compensation every time someone is injured—a system that did that would be a form of "strict liability" and American tort law only imposes strict liability in limited and special cases, which we will take up near the end of this book. The rules of the negligence tort tell us when the victim of an accident is entitled to compensation; when, in other words, the cost of the accident will be shifted from the victim to the person who caused the injury. They reflect social judgments about how to reduce the number and severity of accidents to manageable levels and about when compensation is appropriate, but negligence law does not aspire to eliminate all injuries.

As we shall see, negligence rules operate at a very high level of generality. In other words, they apply uniformly to all of the very varied activities people can undertake. You can inadvertently injure someone (or their property) when you drive your car, when you perform brain surgery, when you ski down a hill, when you serve hot coffee to guests in your apartment, when you chop down a tree in your back yard, and when you operate a restaurant, hair salon or any other sort of business. The legal system uses the same set of rules to determine liability in all of these cases. This makes negligence a very broad, and a very important legal concept. Alas, it also makes it a bit mushy. Rules designed to cover all these varied situations will necessarily be very general, and a bit vague. There can be times when it seems like courts are not really following legal rules at all, but merely flying by the seat of their pants.

Despite this apparent ambiguity, there is a coherent structure to the law of negligence, and a host of sub-rules that build on that foundation. Let us begin with our usual starting point—a list of the elements that an injured plaintiff must prove in order to make out a *prima facie* case for the tort of negligence.

Traditionally, there are five elements to negligence. They are (1) showing that the defendant owes a "duty of care" to the plaintiff and specifying just what that duty of care requires under the facts of the case at issue; (2) showing that the defendant "breached" or failed to live up to, the duty of care; (3) showing that the breach "factually caused" the plaintiff's harm; (4) showing that the plaintiff's harm was within the defendant "scope of legal responsibility" which is often known under the label "proximate cause"; and (5) showing that the plaintiff suffered some damage. The short form version of this list is Duty-Breach-Factual Causation-Proximate Causation-Damages. Elements number three and four are sometimes combined into a single requirement—that the plaintiff prove "causation" though we will be keeping them separate in our discussion to avoid confusion.

Just one additional note on terminology before we go much further. The word "negligence" can be used by courts, text writers, and law professors in two different ways. First, it is the name of a cause of action—the "tort of negligence"—which we will be exploring for the next several chapters. Second, however, it is also a synonym for "breach of duty," which is the second element of the claim. In other words, under this usage, negligence is one element of the tort of negligence! How annoying is that? The only real way to know which meaning is intended is to look to context. In the remainder of this book, I will be as clear as possible to let you know which way I am using the term. You will have to be alert, however, when reading other materials on the law of torts, because other authors may not be as considerate as yours truly.

2. The Concept of a "Duty of Care"

As we have noted, potential injury to persons or property is a byproduct of action. While we cannot eliminate all chance of such injury, we each can reduce the probability of injury by changing the way we act. So, instead of allowing us to behave as we might choose to behave in an empty world, the law obligates us to adhere to a certain minimum standard of behavior to lower the chance of collateral injuries. To put this more formally, we are all obligated to take "risk-reducing precautions" whenever we act. This is what we mean by a "duty of care," or the duty element in the law of negligence. It is a legally imposed requirement that we take some specified amount of care when we act. If we fail to do so, and if that failure causes an injury, we will be obligated to pay those who we injure.

Thinking about the duty element of the negligence tort this way should immediately suggest a follow-up question. If the law mandates that we all take "risk reducing precautions," how much and what kinds of precautions does it mandate? What exactly is it that we each must do when driving our car, going hunting, operating a factory or playing tennis, in order to satisfy our obligation and therefore avoid liability? In other words, what are the specifics of the duty of care?

One could imagine a legal system where the answer to that question would be a long list of highly detailed behavioral requirements. For instance, there could be a statute that said when driving a car the driver must observe a list of, let's say, 54 precautions. These might include such things as turning on headlights when it is raining, refraining from prescription medications before getting in the vehicle, always signaling before changing lanes, checking the tire pressure at least once a month, and on and on. If a driver failed to observe any item on the list and that failure caused an injury to someone, this approach would require the driver to pay damages to the injured party. There would be a comparable list for every other activity imaginable. The problem is that no matter how long and detailed we made the lists, there are likely to be a large number of things we didn't think of. As you may have noticed in reading torts cases, there are an almost infinite number of ways people can come up with to cause an accident.

Consequently, the law has opted for almost the exact opposite approach. Instead of a laundry-list of minute behavioral commands, it has specified the duty of care in the form of a single, all-purpose rule that governs no matter what activity is involved and under all the myriad conditions in which an activity might be performed.

3. The Reasonably Prudent Person Standard of Care

In the typical negligence case, the law requires everyone in society to exercise what is often called "ordinary care." That means that each of us must act with the same degree of care as would be used by a hypothetical ***reasonably prudent person acting under similar circumstances.*** The most recent version of the Restatement of Torts uses a slightly different formulation, phrasing the duty as an obligation to use ***reasonable care under all the circumstances*** (hereinafter RPP or "reasonable care"). There is no substantive difference in the alternative wording, and courts around the country sometimes use their own minor variations in phrasing that differ from both of the versions in this paragraph.

This duty-rule—also referred to as a "standard of care"—applies automatically and in every case, unless it is displaced by some alternative standard (which could be either more or less demanding) or unless the case is one where there is no duty at all. Since the RPP rule governs unless supplanted, we can refer to it as the "default" standard of care. The point is important enough to quote the somewhat dry language of the Restatement for reinforcement:

> *(a) An actor ordinarily has a duty to exercise reasonable care when the actor's conduct creates a risk of physical harm.*
>
> *(b) In exceptional cases, when an articulated countervailing principle or policy warrants denying or limiting liability in a particular class of cases, a court may decide that the defendant has no duty or that the ordinary duty of reasonable care requires modification.*

Restatement (Third) of Torts: Phys. & Emot. Harm § 7 (2010). This section of the Restatement goes on to note (in comment b.) that "a *defendant* has the procedural obligation to raise the issue of whether a no-duty rule or some other modification of the ordinary duty of reasonable care applies in a particular case." [emphasis added]

There are at least two aspects of this RPP or default duty rule that are worth exploring. First, note the reference to "similar circumstances" or "all the circumstances." It is this phrasing that gives the default standard its enormous flexibility. If you were to ask your non-lawyer relatives whether they should drive the same way on a dry sunny day in light traffic and on a day when there is a heavy snow falling, they would no doubt reply, "absolutely not—you should be much more careful on the snowy day." A lawyer, however, would say that you should drive the same way on both occasions—you should act reasonably *given the circumstances.* If the circumstances include limited visibility and icy road conditions, you should take that into account in the way you drive, but semantically or verbally, the standard remains unchanged. The *amount* of care varies depending on the circumstances, but the *standard* of care is fixed and unchanging—be reasonable under the circumstances.

The significance of this point can be seen in a number of cases involving parties who were confronted with a "sudden emergency" not of their own making. For instance, a car darts into a crowded lane of traffic forcing a bus driver to slam on his brakes, which throws a passenger to the floor of the bus, causing her to break an arm. When the passenger sues the bus driver, the defendant-driver might request a special "sudden emergency" jury instruction, which informs the jury that the defendant is not obligated to use the same care and accuracy of choice as one who has time to deliberate.

This is, of course, nothing more than saying that the care expected is reasonable care *under the circumstances*. One is not expected to use the same *amount* of care driving a bus in the middle of an emergency that one would use under more placid conditions because the *circumstances* are different. As the Restatement (Third) puts it: "If an actor is confronted with an unexpected emergency requiring rapid response, this is a circumstance to be taken into account in determining whether the actor's resulting conduct is that of the reasonably careful person." Consequently, many courts have held that the sudden emergency instruction is redundant of the general standard of care. Indeed, quite a few have characterized it as "disfavored" and have said that it should not be used.

Alas, things are never what they seem. Although the default RPP standard refers to "all the circumstances," there are some circumstances that are not taken into account in thinking about the duty of care. For instance, how are you obligated to drive your car when you are drunk? Given that the rule is "drive reasonably under the circumstances," you might think that you have to drive like a reasonable drunk. That would, however, be preposterous. Under such an interpretation you could be mowing down pedestrians right and left and yet have no liability to pay for their damages.

As your common sense should tell you, therefore, drunkenness is not a "circumstance" that "counts" for the purposes of applying the default standard of care. It is disregarded—the drunk driver must drive as carefully as one who is sober, and if he doesn't, he will be liable to those he injures. At least part of the explanation for this result is that the drinker has control over whether to get drunk. A "circumstance" that the defendant causes or can control is not one that is taken into account in interpreting the duty standard. To take an even more obvious example, if Desiree puts on a blindfold before getting into her car, she cannot argue that she is only obliged to drive like a reasonable person who cannot see the road! Moreover, in these cases, we can say that wearing a blindfold (or getting drunk before driving) is itself a failure to act reasonably under the circumstances.

Another group of circumstances that "don't count" are those involving reduced mental or intellectual abilities or skills of the defendant. An ignorant person, one who is stupid, one who is developmentally disabled, or one who is mentally ill is obligated to behave the same way as a sane person of average intelligence. The same point applies to one who is engaged in an activity for the very first time, or lacks experience—the novice skier, for instance, or the person out hunting for the first time in his life.

This is largely for the protection of the rest of us. I don't know if the driver in the next lane is smart or stupid, sane or insane. Since I live in Washington, I might assume that he is indeed stupid or insane, but I don't know for sure. If such persons could avoid liability by showing that they were "doing the best they could" given their mental shortcomings, I would have to drive extremely cautiously. That would be a burden on me and a burden on society. We can sum all this up by saying that when the

RPP standard refers to "circumstances" it is referring to circumstances external to the defendant, such as the weather, not to attributes of the defendant such as intelligence or mental health.

Which takes us to the second key point about the RPP duty standard. The standard is *objective*. It applies to everyone in society exactly the same way. As the rules about mental ability reveal, it does not make any allowances for individual differences. Indeed, in some cases, it demands that certain defendants do the impossible! A foolish person will be held liable for not acting like his more intelligent neighbors, and if he argues that he was incapable of doing so, that argument will be ignored.

There are, however, some exceptions to this rule of objectivity and this tendency to ignore internal attributes of the defendant in applying the RPP standard. One exception involves defendants who have superior skill, knowledge, or intelligence. They are expected to use that additional ability as they engage in various activities. For instance, assume that Diedra, who is a pharmacist, is entertaining her house guest Peggy, who complains of both a head and stomach ache after dinner. Diedra gives Peggy two pills, one for each ailment. There is nothing on the package suggesting that these pills should not be taken together and the typical layperson would not hesitate to take them together. However, Diedra should know, because of her training, that when taken together the pills can cause a serious reaction. Under the traditional duty of care, Diedra was obligated to use this special knowledge, and thus, by giving the pills to the guest, she committed a breach of duty.

Another area where the law departs from an objective approach in interpreting the RPP standard involves the defendant's physical attributes. The hypothetical reasonably prudent person is always assumed to have the same physical characteristics as the defendant. Thus, a blind person is expected to exercise the reasonable care of someone who cannot see; a very tall person is expected to exercise the reasonable care of someone of equally monumental stature; and so on. Of course, physical attributes are not always relevant in a negligence claim. A tall person and a short person should both drive the same way on a snowy afternoon.

The incorporation of superior skill and physical attributes as relevant circumstances under the RPP duty standard is a departure from our usual decision to ignore the internal characteristics of actors. Note, however, that even in these case the *standard* of care remains the same. As the Restatement puts it, "even though the actor's extra skills can properly be considered, these skills do not establish for the actor a standard of care that is higher than reasonable care; rather, they provide a mere circumstance for the jury to consider in determining whether the actor has complied with the general standard of reasonable care." Restatement (Third) of Torts: Phys. & Emot. Harm § 12, cmt a. In other words, it's just that we treat skill and physical attributes as relevant circumstances in applying the universal standard.

Although the RPP duty rule governs in a very large number of cases, it has been found inadequate in a variety of specialized situations. Consequently, there are a several duty rules that can displace the RPP rule. The various sections that follow explore the most important of these special duty situations.

4. The Duty of Care of Children

In most states very young children do not owe others any duty of care at all. The cut-off age varies from state to state but usually is somewhere between 4 and 7 years of age. The current version of the Restatement says that children "less than five years of age" are incapable of negligence. So if you are injured by a careless pre-schooler, you are pretty much out of luck insofar as collecting damages for negligence is concerned.

Children over the specified age are expected to exercise some care when engaging in activities, but their duty is framed differently than the basic RPP standard. Children owe the care of a hypothetical child of *similar age, experience, and intelligence, acting under similar circumstances*. This standard is subjective in nature—it will differ for each child in society. Smart children are held to a higher standard than their, ahem, slower peers. Older children are expected to adhere to a more demanding standard than those who are younger. The novice or inexperienced child gets the benefit of a lower standard of care.

There are several justifications for this generous treatment of children. First, it is often stated that children need some freedom to experiment, grow, and learn, so they should be judged by a more flexible standard. Whether the person injured by a 9-year-old "experimenting"—by attempting to drive his bike with one hand—would find that persuasive is, of course, a matter of debate. Second, some authorities note that children generally confine themselves to activities that are not likely to cause a great deal of harm. They tend not to operate Italian cruise ships, oil tankers, or 18-wheel tractor-trailers. Third, the rule is a concession to the reality that children are less able to appreciate risks, maintain attention, and be aware of alternative courses of conduct. Thus, the standard is designed to determine if they have made reasonable choices given their limited capacities.

In virtually all jurisdictions, however, the special standard for children does not apply if the child is engaged in "a dangerous activity that is characteristically undertaken by adults," as the Restatement (Third) puts it. When a child engages in such an adult activity, the child is obligated to use the ordinary RPP standard of "reasonable care under all the circumstances." There is a broad consensus that operating a motorized vehicle is an adult activity, so a teenager driving a car—or a piece of farm equipment, a motor boat, a snowmobile, or a jet ski—will be judged by the default duty standard. Some cases have found other activities—such as hunting or using firecrackers—to also be adult activities, but the case, are few in number and the states often cannot agree about how to categorize these activities.

5. The Duty of Care of Professionals

Negligence claims against professional service providers are usually called "malpractice" suits. Although such a claim could be asserted against any professional—a lawyer, an accountant, an architect, or an engineer for instance—the bulk of the cases involve suits against health care providers. At the outset, you may wonder why a special duty rule is required in malpractice cases. Couldn't the law just demand that a doctor (or dentist or chiropractor or podiatrist) behave reasonably under the circumstances?

Well, of course it could, but that would lead to a significant problem. The jury is the institution charged with applying the duty rule (or standard of care, as we have been referring to it in the alternative). The general RPP duty rule instructs the jury to compare the defendant's actual conduct to a theoretical or hypothetical standard—that of the imaginary reasonably prudent person. Where the activity is relatively routine, like driving a car, the jury can be trusted to have a good sense of what reasonable care might mean and how the hypothetical reasonably prudent person ought to have behaved under the circumstances of the case.

In the case of specialized professions, however, the jury is likely to lack information about how various activities "should" be performed. The jury consists of a cross-section of the community—a computer programmer, a construction worker, an advertising executive, a school bus driver, and a stay-at-home mom. They almost certainly do not have any information about how a "reasonable" surgeon performs an operation. Let me put it this way: Do you know how to remove a spleen? Me neither. Even if reasonableness were defined in terms of a proper balancing of costs and benefits—an approach we will consider in the next chapter dealing with the breach element—the members of the jury would be in no position to weigh the costs and benefits of various alternative procedures that might be used by a professional.

Consequently, in malpractice cases, the standard of care instructs the jury to compare the defendant *not* with a theoretical or hypothetical standard, but with the defendant's *real world colleagues*. As the Restatement puts it, "one who undertakes to render services in the practice of a profession or trade is required to exercise the skill and knowledge normally possessed by members of that profession or trade in good standing in similar communities."[1]

There are a number of alternative ways different courts around the country phrase this standard, but they all amount to the same thing. Some courts say that a professional must use the same care as the "average member" of the profession. Others say the "custom of the profession" sets the standard of care. Essentially this amounts to a requirement that each professional conform to the group consensus on how to render the services in question.

---

1 Restatement (Second) of Torts § 299A. The more recent Restatement (Third) does not address the issue of professional malpractice.

This still leaves the question of the jury. By itself, this reformulation does not really solve the problem of jury ignorance about professional methodology. The missing link is that under this standard, the plaintiff must, in virtually all cases, call an expert witness who will testify about the prevailing professional custom. Note that this witness does not testify about his or her own way of doing things. That would be legally irrelevant. We don't care about how Dr. Smith takes out a spleen. Rather, we ask Dr. Smith if she knows how most doctors take out spleens, and if she says that she does, she will explain that method to the jury.

There is another aspect of the Restatement version of the professional standard of care that requires our attention. If you go back and look at the quote from that venerable document you will see that there is a reference to "similar communities." Decades ago, courts assumed that small-town or rural doctors did not have the same resources, equipment or perhaps even education, skill, and sophistication as their big city colleagues. To avoid holding them to an impossible standard many states required that the relevant professional custom in a malpractice suit would have to be the custom prevailing in "similar" locales. If the defendant was a doctor from rural Wyoming, an expert from rural Wyoming, or perhaps from a desolate part of upstate New York, would be qualified to explain the customary practice of doctors to the jury, but not some city slicker doctor from New York City or Los Angeles. This was known as the locality rule (or more precisely the "modified" locality rule, since the expert did not have to come from the exact same locality as the defendant, just a similar one).

Of course, advances in technology have made the assumption at the heart of the modified locality rule nearly obsolete. Even smaller town doctors can usually get a patient to an MRI machine or a major trauma center very quickly—we have helicopters and jet planes. Doctors in even the most rural communities have Internet connections and can access the most up-to-the-minute medical journal articles, and even consult with talented colleagues all over the world. As a result, most states have abandoned the locality rule *for specialists*. A brain surgeon in rural Wyoming is not allowed to use a branding iron and a pair of spurs to remove a brain tumor. He will be held to the custom of other brain surgeons nationwide. For primary care doctors and other generalists, about half the states have also gone to the national standard, while the other half retain either a strict or modified locality rule.

The duty approach we have just reviewed in the medical context also governs when any other profession is at issue. An accountant must audit a large company with the "skill and knowledge" of other accountants. In other words, he must conform to the professional custom. In a malpractice suit against him, plaintiff will need an expert witness to testify as to the customary practice of other accountants. Ditto for the lawyer litigating a complex securities fraud case, and the architect designing a new skyscraper.

There is, however, one interesting exception. Education professionals—that is to say, teachers—owe their students no duty of care at all. Zero. Zip. No matter how bad they teach, they cannot be held liable for negligence. The usual rationale for this rule is that it is too difficult to determine whether bad teaching or other factors (such as, perhaps, student stupidity) are the real cause of any subsequent poor outcomes in the job market or elsewhere in life. So if the foregoing paragraphs had you drafting a complaint against one of your first-year professors, you are out luck, and you can toss your draft in the trash.

Before we leave the subject of professional duties, we must consider an additional obligation that is imposed on physicians, and only physicians. This special duty rule is generally known as the doctrine of "informed consent." Under this doctrine, a doctor must inform a patient—prior to commencing a medical procedure—of the risks of that procedure, its necessity, and alternative forms of treatment. Failure to disclose the required information is treated as negligence (in the sense of "breach of duty") and if the undisclosed risk materializes, the patient will have a valid claim against the doctor. There is some disagreement among jurisdictions about whether the required disclosure must consist of information that is commonly disclosed by other doctors—a medical custom approach —or of all information that would be considered important or "material" by a patient.

There are also a number of recognized exceptions to the duty of disclosure imposed by the informed consent doctrine. A doctor need not disclose information that is common knowledge—for instance, that there is likely to be pain or discomfort after major surgery. There is also no duty to make disclosure to a patient who lacks capacity to understand the information, though in these cases, there is a duty to disclose to a guardian who can make a meaningful decision on behalf of the patient. There is also no duty to disclose in cases of emergency. Most controversially, some courts say there is no duty to disclose if disclosure would be medically harmful to the patient. This is controversial because it could lead to circular reasoning. A doctor might think "this patient really needs the operation, but if I disclose the risks, that might scare the patient into denying consent, which would be harmful to the patient, so I have a right to omit the disclosure." The result is that academic writers have argued for a narrow construction of this so-called "therapeutic" exception.

As a practical matter, most physicians have developed written consent forms that they require patients to sign before going ahead with a medical procedure of any complexity. These documents are usually lengthy and quite frightening, as they list a host of truly horrific risks associated with even the most routine procedures. Whether patients read them, and whether they influence anyone's decision is an interesting question.

Some plaintiffs have argued that the medical disclosure duties should extend beyond risks of procedures and the nature of alternatives. For instance, in one case, a doctor failed to tell a patient that the patient had a very short time left to live. As a result the patient did not put his financial affairs in order, which lad to financial detriment for his family. Nonetheless, a California court refused to impose a duty to disclose this sort of information. In another case, a doctor allegedly misrepresented his level of experience—claiming to have performed a type of surgery far more often than he really had done so. While a New Jersey court held that a doctor could be held liable for fraud in the case of an outright lie, it stressed that there was no general duty to disclose experience levels.

6. Duties of Possessors of Land (Premises Liability)

Land ownership has been considered a privileged status in the Anglo-American legal system from at least medieval times. In the modern era, economically minded observers have argued that property owners should be given some protection from liability as an incentive to develop their land and to encourage them to open the land up to others. In the law of negligence this has meant that the duties imposed on those in possession of real estate have, in many cases, been less demanding than the general RPP standard of care.

To be sure you appreciate the sweep of the rules we will explore in this section, bear in mind that "real estate" includes land and structures of all types. It could, in other words, mean an undeveloped tract of rural land, a field on a farm, or a vacant lot in an urban area. It could involve a suburban home along with the surrounding yard and lawn, or an apartment in a high rise building. It could include a retail store and its parking lot, an airport terminal, a shopping mall, or a house of worship. For ease of reference we can call all these various types of real estate "land."

The special duty rules that we consider in this section generally apply to the person who is *in possession* of the land. That may, but need not, be the owner. For instance, many retail stores are in possession of a tenant, as is the case for most rental apartments. In these cases we are interested in specifying the duty of the tenant in the store or apartment should he, she, or it, get sued for negligence.

Although the traditional duty rules for land-possessors are somewhat intricate, you should know at the beginning of the story that about half the states do not use these special rules any longer! Starting with a famous California decision called *Rowland v. Christian,* many states decided that land-possessors should be held to the default standard of care—namely reasonable care under all the circumstances. Whether you need to be familiar with much of the detail that follows thus depends on where you plan to practice and, frankly, the preferences of your instructor.

On the assumption that some readers are either interested in, or obligated to master, the traditional rule structure, let us dive in. The common law duty rules that evolved in this area distinguished between the duty owed by a land-possessor to those who were *off the premises* and the duty owned to those who came on the premises, usually called *entrants.* We will tackle the rules owed to those off the premises first.

Ordinarily, land possessors owe the ordinary duty of a reasonably prudent person to those off the land. If you keep a window box filled with clay flower pots outside your third story apartment window, you must take reasonable precautions to insure that the flower pots are adequately secured. If one falls and beans a passing pedestrian, the question at trial will be the same as in a routine auto accident case, namely whether you exercised reasonable care.

One limitation on this principle, however, is that there is no duty to take steps to alter "natural conditions" on the land to prevent harm to persons outside the property. Under this rule, if you own a hilly parcel of land adjacent to a road and rocks sometimes slide from your property onto that road after a heavy rain, you have no duty to build a fence or take any other steps to prevent that from happening and no responsibility to drivers who may get hurt by falling rocks.

To make things more interesting (which is the way a law professor says "more complicated"), however, there is an exception to this exception. We can call this curlicue the "urban tree" rule. It declares that a possessor of land located in an urban area must use reasonable care to protect persons using a public road from harm from trees on his land. Many of the cases actually involve this sub-rule. Typical fact patterns involve letting trees grow so that they obscure road signs or road hazards, and failing to prune or cut down diseased trees so that limbs eventually fall into the road or directly onto passing cars. Because reasonable care governs in this type of case, once again, the effect is to treat the situation like any other negligence suit involving the RPP rule.

As mesmerizing as the urban tree cases may be, litigation involving injuries to persons who actually enter the property is far more common. Such suits are often called "premises liability" suits for the obvious reason that the injury occurs "on the premises" possessed by the defendant. The traditional duty rules in such cases turned on two issues: (a) what was the entrant's legal status on the land and (b) was the entrant injured by activities being conducted by the defendant on the premises, or by a static condition on the property.

Where the entrant is a trespasser, and the possessor has no knowledge of his presence on the land and no reason to expect him to be there, the traditional common law rule imposed no duty at all, regardless of how the injury was caused. The Restatement (Second) offers some illuminating examples in § 333. It notes that if a possessor sets traps in his woodlands to capture predators which are killing his game animals, the possessor will not be liable to a trespasser who is injured by a trap, even if it would have taken little effort to post a warning and a reasonable person would thus have given that warning. This would be a case of injury to an unknown trespasser via a dangerous condition. The Restatement also notes that a possessor hunting on his own land is not liable for accidentally shooting a trespasser he did not see, even one "whose presence [he] could have discovered if had taken even the slightest pains to do so." This would be a case of injury via activities conducted by the defendant-possessor. All this can be summed up with the pithy observation that an unknown trespasser always loses a premises liability under the traditional rule because he is never owed any sort of duty of care.

Some courts use a slightly different formulation in cases involving unknown trespassers. They say that the duty to such an entrant is only to refrain from wilful, wanton, or reckless conduct. This is, however, just another way of saying that there would be no liability for ordinary negligence. One who acts wilfully—for instance by deliberately shooting a visible trespasser—

is of course liable, but the proper claim would be battery, not negligence. Similarly, reckless or "wanton" conduct reflects an extreme degree of indifference to the welfare of others. This leaves the door open a crack to allow the unknown trespasser to recover in cases where the behavior of the possessor truly shocks the conscience.

When the possessor is aware of the presence of the trespasser, or where there has been constant trespassing on a limited part of the property so that future trespassing should be expected, the no-duty-at-all approach no longer applies. In this scenario, the possessor is obligated to carry on *activities* with reasonable care. Many of the cases involve railroads, or their urban equivalent, subway systems. Passenger are, obviously, not allowed on the tracks and if they go on the tracks, they are trespassers. Once the engineer sees someone on the tracks, however, the engineer must exercise reasonable care under the circumstances to avoid injury. Of course, if the engineer only sees the trespasser at the very last minute, reasonable care *under the circumstances* may not do the person on the tracks any good—it may be too late to stop the train no matter what is done.

In cases involving known trespassers who encounter hazardous conditions on the land, the traditional rules introduced yet another distinction—between conditions which are natural to the land and those that are artificial. For the former, no duty is imposed at all. Thus there would be no duty to protect a known trespasser from an accumulation of ice on your back porch, and if such a person slipped on the ice, you would have no liability.

Where the condition is artificial, the Restatement says there is only a duty to a known trespasser where the condition involves a "risk of death or serious bodily harm" and the trespasser is unlikely to discover the danger on his own. Some courts revert again to the "refrain from willful, wanton or reckless" formulation in this known-trespasser-artificial-condition scenario, which as a practical matter, amounts to the same thing. An example might be if employees of a commuter rail line see people hiking along the tracks in close proximity to a concealed electrified third rail. Since the third rail is a highly dangerous artificial condition, since the employees are aware of the presence of the trespassing hikers, and since the hikers are unlikely to discover the danger on their own, the employees would owe the hikers a duty to protect them from harm. If the employees did nothing and the hikers were injured, the employees (and the rail line) would be liable in a negligence suit.

The next type of entrant we encounter is known as a licensee. This is a person who enters the land with the consent of the possessor, but who is not there to conduct business, and is not a member of the general public. The typical licensee is a social guest. With respect to activities being conducted on the property, the possessor owes a licensee the ordinary or default duty of the RPP. Thus, if you invite a few friends over for a backyard barbecue and decide to have a game of lawn darts, you must be reasonably prudent in the manner in which you throw the darts to avoid planting one in the forehead of one of your guests.

With regard to conditions, a possessor must exercise reasonable care to protect the licensee only when the condition is concealed from the licensee and the possessor knows, or has reason to know, of that condition. There is, however, no duty to inspect the property to discover other hazards. This idea is sometimes captured in the saying that the licensee takes the property "on the same basis" as the possessor. If you don't know that your balcony railing is loose, you have no obligation to protect your social guests from the danger it poses and will not be held liable in a negligence suit if they lean on it and plummet 15 floors to the pavement.

The final category of entrants on land are invitees. A person is an invitee if they enter premises with permission and for a business purpose, or if the premises are held open to the general public. That means you are an invitee when you enter your local supermarket or barber shop, and also an invitee when you enter a museum or church (presuming you do so during regular hours when the facility or store is open). The possessor of premises must conduct all activities with reasonable care to avoid injuring invitees and, if he or his employees fail to use reasonable care, they are liable for injuries that they cause. This means, as we have observed previously when the duty is reasonable care, that the cases of this sort do not differ at all from routine negligence litigation.

Regarding protection of invitees from hazardous conditions, the possessor must take steps to avoid injury from all conditions that are concealed from the invitee if the possessor either knows of the condition in advance, or could have discovered the condition through a reasonable inspection. For instance, assume that Porter, a member of a swim club, is exiting the pool via a metal ladder when the ladder detaches from the side of the pool, causing Porter to get hurt. If he can prove that a reasonable swim club would have been aware of the problem through a program of reasonable inspections, he will be entitled to recover in a negligence suit for his injuries. On the other hand, if the club did not know of the danger and could not have discovered it via a reasonable inspection, poor Porter will be out of luck.

You might think that these rules require land-possessors to spend a lot of money repairing all sorts of hazards on their land. That is not necessarily the case. Whenever a duty exists in favor of a particular entrant with respect to a condition, that duty can be discharged *either* by making the condition safe, *or* by giving a warning. A warning satisfies the duty of care because it puts the entrant on notice about the danger and allows him to protect himself. Of course, a warning would have to be sufficiently prominent and clear to serve the purpose of alerting the entrant, and whether any given warning passes that test can be a subject of dispute at trial.

A corollary of this principle is that there is usually no duty to protect entrants from "open and obvious dangers." Such hazards provide their own warning. If the owner of a sawmill invites a prospective purchaser of lumber to tour the mill, he does not have to warn the visitor not to rest his forehead on the buzzing circular blades. Of course, this rule is interpreted flexibly. If a hazard is in plain view, but the entrant is likely to be distracted, or if the entrant has no way to avoid encountering the hazard, courts will often hold that the possessor should have done more, and impose liability for negligence if he did not.

As if all this weren't complex enough, there are some special rules that apply when the case involves trespassing children. A possessor of land must exercise reasonable care to prevent trespassing children from being injured by dangerous artificial conditions on the land if trespassing is foreseeable and if children would not be likely to appreciate the danger for themselves.

The earliest cases of this sort involved children entering railroad yards and getting hurt on railroad turntables. These are large rotating circular tables set in the ground with a small bit of railroad track in the middle. When a locomotive is driven onto the table, the table can be spun around to change the direction of travel. Because the tables rotate they are fun to play on. Unfortunately, little limbs are sometimes caught in the space between the table and the enclosure, with resulting tragic consequences. To get around the defendant's argument that they should not be liable because the traditional rule imposes no duty to a trespasser, courts reasoned that the child had been lured onto the land by the prospect of playing with the apparatus, and that therefore he was in some sense, invited onto the land. In other words, his trespasses should be forgiven. This favorable rule for child trespassers is sometimes called the "attractive nuisance" doctrine because of this logic.

To say that all these various rules governing premises liability cases are baroque is both to understate the matter and to insult all things baroque. It is little wonder that, as noted at the beginning of the section, many states have thrown the whole thing in the trash and decided that all negligence suits against land possessors should be litigated under the basic reasonable prudence duty rule. Of course, that rule requires reasonable care *under the circumstances* and courts following the modern view still consider whether the plaintiff entered with or without permission, whether the plaintiff was a child, whether the injury was caused by an activity or a condition, and whether the condition was natural or artificial to be *circumstances* relevant to determining whether the possessor acted reasonably. While it may be "reasonably prudent" to allow a herd of bison to roam free on your property if it is an unoccupied 5,000 acre parcel in the middle of rural Nebraska, that would likely not be prudent if you were running a day care center for pre-schoolers in suburban Washington, D.C.

7. Duties Based on Criminal Statutes

As I hope you recall, early in this chapter I suggested that one way the legal system could have dealt with the issue of duty would have been to promulgate detailed codes of behavior for a large variety of common activities. Negligence law, as we saw, typically shuns that approach in favor of the generality of the RPP standard. However, there is another field of law which positively overflows with specific rules of behavior—the criminal law.

In many negligence cases, plaintiffs point to the requirements of a criminal statute and ask the court to treat those requirements as a highly specific duty command. In other words, these plaintiffs seek to "borrow" a criminal statute, even though it technically has no applicability to personal injury litigation, and turn it into a one-time-only substitute for the reasonably prudent person standard of care. Let us posit an example to make the conversation a bit more concrete.

Every jurisdiction has a law that requires motorists to stop at a red traffic light. The consequence of failing to obey that law is penal—you get a ticket and unless the jurisdiction is oddly strict about traffic laws, you pay a fine. On its face, the statute has no implications whatsoever for the tort system—it does not say that failure to stop at a red light obligates you to pay damages to any pedestrians or motorists who you may injure.

A negligence plaintiff who has been hit by a car while crossing the street may, however, ask the judge to use the substantive part of the statute (as opposed to its penalty provisions) as a declaration of duty in his particular negligence suit. If the judge agrees to do that, the jury will be instructed that the defendant had a duty "to stop at the red light," rather than the generic duty to "exercise reasonable care under all the circumstances." Moreover, the jury will be told that if they find that the defendant did not stop at the red light, they should treat that fact as *negligence per se.* (In this usage, the word negligence is a synonym for the breach element—proof of violation of the statute would be conclusive evidence of a breach of duty).

This leaves us with the heart of the matter: *When* will a court agree to borrow a criminal statute and use its terms as a specific duty of care? The traditional answer is that the court will do so when plaintiff can make a two-part showing. First, plaintiff must show that he is a member of the class of persons that the statute is trying to protect. Second, the plaintiff must show that the accident which occurred is within the class of risks that the statute is trying to prevent.

In the case of the red light statute, application of the test does not require much intellectual heavy lifting. Such statutes are clearly designed to protect persons crossing the street (along with drivers and passengers in cars moving perpendicular to the red light), and it is designed to protect them from the risk of . . . well, being hit by cars. In many auto accident cases where the plaintiff alleges that the immediate cause of the accident was a traffic violation, you can anticipate that the relevant traffic statute will become the standard of care.

In other cases of course, figuring out who a criminal statute is intended to protect or what risks the legislature was worried about when it adopted the statute can be much more speculative. For instance, assume that there is a statute that forbids the sale of ammunition to a minor. If a merchant sells a teenager some bullets in violation of that law, and the purchaser then uses them to commit suicide, should a court borrow the "don't-sell-bullets-to-a-minor" law and use it as the standard of care in a negligence claim against the vendor? One might argue that the statute seeks to protect *others* who might be shot by a poorly trained and immature minor using a weapon, in which case the suicide victim would not be in the class of persons that the statue seeks to protect. On the other hand, the legislature may have been thinking about the suicide scenario when it passed the law. There may be some hints about this issue in the legislative history, but there is often no way to know for sure, and courts are often left to make their best guess.

In some jurisdictions courts do not treat the violation of a statute meeting the two-part test as negligence (breach) per se. Rather, under this minority view, the statutory violation is merely some evidence of negligence. This permits the plaintiff to introduce evidence of the statute's existence, and argue the violation to the jury as significant proof that the defendant behaved unreasonably, but it permits the defendant to offer evidence of other surrounding circumstances that arguably made his conduct reasonable on the occasion involved.

Even in jurisdictions that follow the majority rule there are a number of exceptions to the negligence per se doctrine. When these exceptions govern, courts decline to use the statute as the standard of care, and instead instruct the jury to apply the default RPP duty standard.

The first exception arises in cases where a party could not comply with a statute because of an incapacity. For instance, a statute that requires certain conduct upon seeing a particular hazard might not be used by a court to set the standard of care for a visually impaired person who was incapable of seeing that hazard. Another exception exists if the eventual defendant did not know, and should not have known, of the occasion for compliance. A classic but dated illustration here is a driver who is unaware that one of his tail lights has gone out while he is in the middle of a journey. Today, of course, many cars would have a dashboard indicator informing the driver of the problem.

A third exception arises when a party is unable, after reasonable diligence, to comply with the statute. For instance, perhaps a statute might require shopkeepers to shovel the sidewalk in front of their premises within 24 hours after snow stops falling. If there has been a severe blizzard that would make manual shoveling of snow impossible and if obtaining a snow-blower would take several days because of the high demand, compliance with the statute might be excused. A fourth recognized exception involves cases where a sudden emergency prevents statutory compliance. For instance, a driver might swerve over the center line of a highway—in violation of a statute that forbids that act—to avoid hitting a child who darts in front of her car.

Finally, a statute will not be used as a duty standard if compliance with the statute would be more dangerous than violation. In one well-known case, a statute required pedestrians walking on the side of a highway to walk on the left side so that they would face approaching traffic. Although the pedestrians in that case violated the statute by walking on the right side of the road, there was very heavy traffic on the left side and much lighter traffic on the right. The court thus found their non-compliance with the statute to be excused.[2]

8. The No-Duty-To-Rescue Rule

You can find, in many books on Tort law, a statement that there is "no duty to act affirmatively." This may, at first blush, seem puzzling. If a driver is approaching a red light, the ordinary duty of care—as well as the duty based on the traffic code—requires the driver to engage in the "affirmative act" of lifting his foot from the gas pedal, placing it on the brake, and pressing

2 The pedestrians in that case were the victims and eventual plaintiffs. They were accused of *contributory* negligence per se by the driver who hit them. The case alluded to is *Tedla v. Ellman*, 280 N.Y. 124, 19 N.E.2d 987 (1939).

down with enough pressure to stop the car before entering the intersection. So what, then, does it mean, to say that there is no duty to "act affirmatively"?

The slogan is essentially just a sloppy way of saying that the rules of negligence law regulate *how* you must conduct an activity, but they do not obligate you *to undertake the activity in the first instance*. If you go hunting you must hunt as a reasonably prudent person, but you are not obligated to go hunting. If you opt to practice medicine you must observe the professional standard of care and use the same skill and knowledge as other professionals, but you are not forced to go to medical school and then engage in the practice of medicine.

The most frequently analyzed consequence of this no-duty rule is that individuals are not obligated to come to the aid of a person in peril, even if they can do so with virtually no effort or risk to themselves. This is often summed up in the pithy, albeit heartless, phrase that there is "no duty to rescue." The Restatement illustration reveals the cruel and callous potential of this rule with eye-popping clarity:

> *A sees B, a blind man, about to step into the street in front of an approaching automobile. A could prevent B from so doing by a word or touch without delaying his own progress. A does not do so, and B is run over and hurt. A is under no duty to prevent B from stepping into the street, and is not liable to B.*

Charming, isn't it?

There are two major exceptions to the no-duty-to-rescue rule. When the defendant has put the plaintiff in peril in the first place or is otherwise the cause of the situation, most courts will impose a duty. This is true even if the defendant's act that caused the peril was not, in the first instance, negligent. For instance, if a motorist hits a hiker on the side of a road—whether because he was driving negligently or due to an innocent and unavoidable accident—he cannot merely leave the victim lying there and continue on his merry way.

Second, where there is a pre-existing relationship between the defendant and the person in peril, the law will also impose a duty. Historically, the concept of a relationship was confined to fairly formal categories, such as those between a common carrier and its passengers, an innkeeper and its guests, or an employer and its employees. Thus, if you are a guest at a hotel and there is a fire in the building, the hotel would owe you a duty to attempt to save you. In recent years, courts have expanded the relationship concept to encompass more informal and casual associations. On this view, if you go out to dinner with a friend, and she stumbles badly on the sidewalk and begins bleeding profusely from her head, you could not simply continue on to dinner without her. Well, you could, but if you did, you would be liable for negligence when she sued you because you owed her a duty of care.

In these situations, once a duty arises it is a duty to act reasonably under the circumstances. Consequently, this duty does not obligate a rescuer to put his or her own life in peril. A reasonable person, in other words, recognizes that there is no profit in trying to save someone else if it is likely that he will get killed in the process. Thus, in the hotel fire case, the "duty to rescue" may obligate hotel staff to call the fire department, but it does not obligate staff to engage in heroics such as dashing through the flames into your guest room and carrying you down 20 flights of stairs.

If one attempts a rescue in a situation where there is no duty, reasonable care is also required. This means that if a gratuitous rescuer rescues in a careless fashion, or abandons the rescue midway through, he or she will be vulnerable to a claim of negligence. Obviously, this rule acts as a significant deterrent to voluntary rescue because anyone who is aware of it will think twice before choosing to play the hero. The reward for the good deed could be liability for significant money damages. To mitigate this consequence many states have passed statutes known as Good Samaritan laws. Such laws immunize rescuers from liability under certain conditions. The details of these statutes vary considerably from state to state. For instance, some only immunize members of specific professions, such as doctors or nurses, while other immunize all members of the public. Some provide a defense against a claim of ordinary negligence but retain liability for gross negligence. Of course most non-lawyers are not likely to be fully informed about the nuances of their local Good Samaritan law and, in this state of ignorance, are thus left to follow their instincts and moral impulses about whether to rescue a stranger in peril, with whatever legal consequence may ensue.

9. Duties to Prevent Emotional Harm

Sometimes a careless defendant does not cause direct physical harm to anyone. Rather, his carelessness may leave someone profoundly shaken emotionally. The question, then, is when will the emotionally injured party be entitled to recover in a negligence claim? As a theoretical matter, the situations when recovery is allowed mark out the boundaries of the duty to avoid inflicting emotional harm. More practically, however, the various rules in this area operate as additional requirements a plaintiff must prove, over and above the fact that the defendant committed some negligent act (such as running a red light, or carelessly aiming his gun in the direction of another member of his hunting party).

Before we have our look at the rules in this area, candor compels me to tell you that the cases are a bit of a mess. There is not only the usual diversity of rules from state to state, but sometimes it is difficult to distill clear rules from the cases even within a single state. In the paragraphs that follow we will try to sort through this confusion.

Essentially, there are three different categories of cases involving negligent infliction of emotion distress, each with its own set of special rules. The first group can be called the "near miss" cases. In these, the defendant's negligent act does not physically harm the plaintiff but it places the plaintiff in a zone of physical danger and, as a result, the plaintiff experiences emotions of fear for his physical safety. For instance, a driver who runs a red light and *almost* hits a pedestrian would be liable in a negligence suit brought by that pedestrian for the anxiety the pedestrian suffered.

In most states, however, in order to recover, the plaintiff in a near miss case must also show that the distress produced some visible physical symptoms—a manifestation of the anxiety that can assure us that the claim is not wholly fabricated. If the pedestrian in a near miss case is so agitated that he has a heart attack, that would certainly qualify. Lesser symptoms of distress might include breaking out in a rash, or developing an uncontrollable muscle spasm. The trend has been towards liberalizing this requirement. Some recent cases, for instance, have held that symptoms of depression satisfy the subsequent harm requirement. Of course, many of the symptoms of depression—such as an inability to concentrate, or loss of interest in one's daily activities—are not objectively observable. Allowing this kind of evidence may therefore seem inconsistent with the desire to prevent false claims. With our increased understanding of mental health, brain chemistry, and psychiatry, however, the fear of fabricated claims may be receding.

A second kind of claim for negligent infliction of emotional distress is the "bystander" claim. In these claims the eventual plaintiff is distressed because of a negligent injury inflicted on another person (whom we can call the "direct victim"). Note that a bystander plaintiff does not experience the emotion of fear that is at the root of the "near miss" cases; rather, the unpleasant emotion produced by the careless defendant is the emotion of grief or sadness at the thought of the injuries suffered by the direct victim.

In order for a plaintiff to prevail in a bystander case, courts require that the plaintiff and the direct victim be close family members, and require that the plaintiff observe the injury to the direct victim as it happens. If a father sees his son run over and killed by a drunk driver, the father will have an emotional distress claim against the driver. If, however, the same man sees his neighbor and best friend run down, he cannot recover, nor could he recover if he learned of the death of his son via a phone call ten minutes after the fatal impact. Both of these rules have been relaxed to some degree by various states. Thus, in some states, persons engaged to be married have been treated as close family members for purposes of a bystander distress claim, and in others recovery is allowed even if the plaintiff did not witness the accident as it happened, so long as he arrives on the scene shortly thereafter.

The various judicial requirements in the bystander scenario are designed to prevent a single episode from resulting in liability to dozens or hundreds of people. If there were no requirement of family relationship, everyone at a busy intersection could assert a claim if they witnessed a pedestrian hit and killed by a drunk driver. If there were no requirement of presence at the scene, every member of a family would have a claim for distress whenever one of them was hurt or killed by a negligent act even if they only learned of the accident weeks after it happened. Indeed, the concern about excessive liability is so great that some states have thrown up additional hurdles in the bystander situation. In New York, the bystander plaintiff must himself be in a zone of physical danger in order to recover. Consequently, one who sees his spouse killed by a negligent act while standing a safe distance away is denied recovery in the Empire State.

The final group of cases we can identify in the area of negligent infliction of emotional distress are the "relationship" cases. Here, the plaintiff and the defendant are in some sort of preexisting business relationship, and it is highly foreseeable that negligence on the part of the defendant-business in performing its functions will cause significant distress to the plaintiff. For instance, a medical lab can predict to a high degree of certainty that if it carelessly gives a patient a false positive cancer diagnosis, that will be very distressing. Similarly, a funeral establishment can predict to a high degree of certainty that negligence in the preparation or display of the remains of a loved one will be very distressing to their customers.

Some courts have confused the relationship cases with the other categories, and have denied recovery for such curious reasons as the fact that the plaintiff was not in a zone of danger created by the defendant's careless act. Of course the acts in these cases usually do not involve a risk of *physical* harm to anyone, making the zone of danger analysis inapt. The better reasoned cases appreciate that these cases are in a category of their own, and seem willing to allow recovery when the plaintiff can prove the foreseeability of the distress and the failure of the defendant to use reasonable care.

10. Duties to Guard Against Harm Caused By Third Parties

Plaintiffs bring negligence cases in order to secure an economic recovery. This means that if they are harmed by a person without any financial resources, they have a strong incentive to look further afield to find a defendant with the proverbial "deep pocket." This has led to a large number of negligence cases where the plaintiff sues a defendant and alleges that the defendant had an obligation (duty) to protect plaintiff from some other person who directly inflicted harm.

For instance, a tavern owner may neglect to "cut off" a visibly intoxicated drunk patron and the patron may then run down the plaintiff on his drive home. The injured party in this case may discover that the drunk driver has no resources and no insurance, and so opt to sue the tavern owner, claiming that he had a duty to "control" the patron by not serving him so much alcohol. To take another example, a school might fail to screen visitors, and a visitor admitted to the building might then assault a pupil. The injured pupil may not be able to find the assailant, who has fled the jurisdiction, and so opts to sue the school, alleging that they should have exercised greater care to control the visitor.

Note that in the tavern case, the "third party" who directly caused injury was negligent (drunk driving) while in the school case the third party acted intentionally (criminal assault). That is of no particular significance. The key point is that in both cases the injured party claims that the party being sued (the tavern-owner or the school) had a duty to exercise control and carelessly failed to do so. The question is when courts are willing to impose a duty in cases of this sort.

Most courts find such a duty if two conditions are met. First, they require that a risk of harm be *foreseeable*. Second, they demand that the eventual defendant have some sort of *relationship* with either the third person who directly inflicts the harm, or with the victim. Let us first consider cases where the relationship that forms the basis of the duty is between the defendant and the source of harm. Several well-established relationships fall into this category.

For instance, parents have a duty to exercise reasonable care to control their children, provided they have the ability to control and knowledge of the need to exercise such control to prevent danger to others (which is another way of saying that harm is foreseeable). The parent's awareness of a need to control might be based on knowledge that the child is in possession of a dangerous object, such as a hunting rifle or powerful fireworks. It could also be based on issues such as the child's temperament, as when the child suffers from a developmental problem that makes him or her aggressive towards strangers. Bear in mind, in cases of this sort, that reasonable parents often let children play outside without supervision, and that reasonable parents cannot and do not hover over their children, monitoring them at every minute. The mere fact that a child intentionally or negligently hurts someone is not, by itself, evidence of parental carelessness. There must be some reason the parent should have anticipated particular harm and some failure to exercise a reasonable precaution before a court will impose liability.

Other relationships where courts normally impose a duty are those between employers and their employees; between land possessors and those legally on the land (meaning both invitees and licensees); and between those who have taken custody over dangerous persons. Thus, in one Iowa case, a 19-year-old was hosting a party at his parents' home. You will be shocked to hear that there was beer involved. According to the court "[a]pproximately two hours after the party began a group of six uninvited males arrived and were admitted to the house." Some of the guests "noticed that the group of men had an 'intimidating look' about them" and suggested to the host that he should ask them to leave. The host, however, did not ask them to leave and, predictably, they assaulted a guest. Because the troublesome group were licensees, the possessor of the property had a duty to prevent them from causing foreseeable harm to others if he could do so through the exercise of reasonable care. Because he failed to do so he was found liable.

The Restatement offers another example that you may find useful: "A operates a private sanatarium for the insane. Through the negligence of the guards employed by A, B, a homicidal maniac, is permitted to escape. B attacks and causes harm to C. A is subject to liability to C." While the typical facility for the mentally ill may not house many "homicidal maniacs," if you do have custody of one, it is surely not reasonably prudent to let him escape and terrorize the neighborhood.

Courts have sometimes imposed a duty to control in situations that do not fit neatly into one of the relationships mentioned thus far, so long as there was a reason to anticipate danger and an ability to prevent it. One classic case is *Tarasoff v. Regents of the University of California.* In that case, a troubled student at Cal Berkeley named Prosenjit Poddar told a campus psychologist named Dr. Moore that he planned to kill a female student who Poddar believed had romantically rebuffed him. Poddar eventually acted on this threat and killed Tatiana Tarasoff. Her family sued Dr. Moore and the University, claiming that they owed Tatiana a duty to protect her from the prospect of (intentional) harm by Poddar. They argued that Moore should have at least given Tarasoff a warning. The California Supreme Court agreed with this claim, imposing a duty of care in this case.

As indicated earlier in this section, a duty can also be based on a relationship between the defendant *and the plaintiff*. Many of these relationships are the same as those just considered. Thus, a defendant who is a land-possessor may owe a duty to exercise reasonable care to protect invitees from dangerous third parties, just as he owes a duty to prevent those invitees from hurting others. Under this rule, a motel might be held negligent for inadequate security that allows an assailant to gain entrance and injure a guest, because of the relationship between the motel and guest. Similarly, a school might owe a duty to its pupils, as would any other institution that takes custody over people for a period of time, such as a hospital, nursing home, or half-way house for persons with mental disabilities. Ditto for an employer, who would owe the duty to employees. Many cases also impose the duty on one member of a family to protect others such as spouses, parents, and children.

Where the third party inflicting harm is a criminal, some courts have attempted to narrow the foreseeability requirement. They hold that before a business can be liable to a customer for failure to protect from a criminal assault, there must have been similar crimes on the property of that particular business. This seems rather artificial, as harm from criminal attacks would seem foreseeable if people have been repeatedly mugged next door, even if no muggings have yet taken place on defendant's property. Consequently, many courts consider what they call "the totality of the circumstances" when analyzing the foreseeability of third-party harm.

11. Duties Owed to Unborn Children

Most of the duty problems we have considered address whether special circumstances (such as the existence of a criminal statute) or the status of the defendant (such as the fact that he is a land-possessor or a doctor) alter the usual duty of care or eliminate it entirely. Sometimes, however, the identity of the *victim* can also be a basis for invoking special duty rules. That is the situation we find when the victim of the tort is an unborn child.[4]

When a negligent defendant causes an injury to a pregnant woman, there is a possibility that the fetus that she is carrying may also be injured as well. The mother-to-be will, of course, have a cause of action in her own name for her own injuries. Whether the unborn child has a separate claim typically depends on whether it is born alive. If the child is born alive, but with injuries or an impairment traceable to the negligent impact on the mother's body, virtually all courts will allow a recovery. Where the child is not born alive—in other words when there is a stillbirth—there is a division of authority. A significant number of states will not allow a wrongful death cause of action by the (administrator of the estate of the) dead baby, though in many of those, the mother may recover additional damages for her emotional distress due to the loss of her expected child in her own claim. On the other hand, a slightly larger number of states do allow the wrongful death case on behalf of the baby to go forward, at least where the fetus was viable at the time of the injury. Some of this variation between the states can be explained by the differences in wording of the wrongful death

---

4 Choosing a term to designate the victim in these cases can be tricky because the label may imply to some readers a position on the emotional question of abortion. I will alternate in this section between the terms fetus and unborn child. Neither term is meant to advance any particular political position on the abortion debate.

statutes, but some of it just reflects different policy judgments about the proper rule choice.

In the medical context, a number of special cases have cropped up that deserve particular mention. One situation involves a negligently conducted diagnostic test. In these cases, a doctor negligently fails to diagnose fetal abnormalities and inform the parents about them. When the child is born the *parents* may claim that they would have terminated the pregnancy had they been given accurate information. This is often called a "wrongful birth" case. About half the states recognize this cause of action. Most of those limit recovery to the extraordinary costs of raising a child with severe birth defects, though some also allow the parents to recover additional sums for their emotional distress. Some states, however, such as Minnesota, Idaho, and Missouri, for instance, view this claim as implicitly endorsing abortion and have consequently forbidden it by statute.

In that same situation the *child* may also assert a claim, usually called a "wrongful life" suit, arguing that if only the doctor had done the diagnostic test correctly, the parents would have ended the pregnancy, meaning that he would never have been born, and thus would not have to endure a life of physical pain and related damages flowing from the birth defects. Only a handful of states allow this claim to go forward, and in some of those, the child's recovery is limited to economic loss (medical expenses during his life necessary to cope with his disability) and do not include pain and suffering. Courts denying the claim reason that the injuries associated with the disability simply cannot be rationally compared with the alternative—the void of non-existence.

One could summarize the results in the wrongful birth and wrongful life cases by saying that a doctor's duty in connection with pre-natal testing for birth defects generally runs only to the parents, and not to the unborn infant. Not all courts, however, choose to put it that way.

A somewhat different situation arises when a doctor negligently performs a sterilization procedure, with the result that the parents conceive a child that they did not expect or want to have. In this case, the parents bring the pregnancy to term, but sue the doctor to recover the economic costs of raising the child. Many courts reject this claim, reasoning that the intangible benefits the child brings to the family outweigh the costs—the pitter-patter of that extra pair of little feet presumably compensating the parents for the extra $200,000 they will have to spend on college tuition. Note that in this type of case, the *child* does not assert a claim on his own behalf since he or she has not suffered any harm from the defendant-doctor's negligence. Indeed, but for the doctor's negligence, the child would never have been born.

12. Duty of Care of the Government

As a child, your humble author recalls sometimes hearing parents or other older relatives conclude some diatribe about alleged government incompetence with the remark, "Well, what are you gonna do? You can't sue City Hall." Turns out they were wrong. You can sue City Hall and sometimes you can even win.

At the outset, you should be aware that there are significant distinctions between the rules that govern suits against the government itself, and suits against individual governmental actors, such as the police officer on the beat. This chapter is limited to a discussion of the former situation (for instance, a suit against the United States of America). There are also some distinctions—less significant but not trivial—between suits against the federal government, suits against state governments, and suits against subdivisions of states such as cities, towns or counties. To keep the conversation streamlined, we will largely ignore those distinctions as well. Finally, in many instances governmental misconduct can implicate various provisions of the Federal Constitution as opposed to conventional common law torts. For those kinds of issues your best bet is to consult a book that treats Constitutional Law.

Until the middle decades of the twentieth century, the doctrine of "sovereign immunity" prevented most tort suits against both the federal government and the states. By the end of the Second World War, however, most jurisdictions had waived their sovereign immunity, opening themselves up to negligence claims. The federal government did that in a statute called the Federal Tort Claims Act (FTCA). However, Congress and the state legislatures limited the scope of their waiver, retaining immunity in a variety of situations.

First, governments generally did *not* waive their immunity for intentional torts. Thus, if you are punched in the face by the clerk at the Social Security Office or, as is much more likely, at the state Department of Motor Vehicles, you may have a battery claim against the clerk, but you will not have any remedy against the government of the United States or of your home state. The FTCA waiver of immunity also does not extend to claims based on defamation, malicious prosecution, abuse of process, or interference with contract. In other words, you cannot sue the United States for a tort because the local U.S. Attorney filed a baseless criminal case against you (recall, however, that there may be a viable Constitutional claim).

Perhaps the most important category of reserved immunity is the one for "discretionary functions." Where a governmental officer is allowed to make a choice, and where that choice is based on considerations of policy, individuals will not have any recourse in court against the government if they are harmed by the choice. For instance, if the superintendent of a National Park decided not to install rustic steps on a hiking path, but rather opted to keep the path unimproved, because of a policy decision to preserve the natural characteristics of the terrain, a hiker who fell on the path would not have a claim against the United States. Even if this decision was not "reasonably prudent" it is a discretionary decision and thus the government is immune from a negligence claim. On the other hand, if a worker at the park simply neglected to clean up a soap spill in a rest room and a park visitor slipped and injured himself, the visitor could pursue a claim. There is no "policy" judgment implicated in the decision about cleaning the rest room.

The FTCA also has a number of special procedural rules that govern in tort suits against the United States. For instance, there is no jury in these cases; the government must be given advance notice of the plaintiff's intent to sue; and there can be no punitive damages. Interestingly, any issue of substantive law in an FTCA suit is based on the law of the state where the accident occurred. Thus, if a careless plaintiff is hurt by a federal employee in one of the few states that denies all recovery under the contributory negligence rule, that plaintiff would be out of luck.

While the rules governing the retained immunity of the states are generally similar, there are a number of other approaches used, depending on the jurisdiction. The topic is a big one. The various nuances are not well suited for a short and happy treatment of tort law and are not usually covered in great depth in the usual first-year survey course in Torts.

13. Family and Charitable Immunity

In former times, members of the same family could not sue each other for torts of any kind. In the context of negligence suits, this amounted to a blanket "no duty of care" rule—no matter how careless you were towards your spouse or children, you could not be held liable for their injuries. There were two traditional justifications for this position. First, there was a concern that allowing intra-family suits would undermine family harmony, pitting husband versus wife or child versus parent as adversaries in a court of law. Second, there was a concern about collusive suits. The fear here was that members of the same family might have an incentive to conjure up fabricated stories of carelessness and injury in order to secure compensation from a liability insurance policy.

Whatever the force of those arguments, the injustice of denying recovery to a person riding in a car driven by his or her negligent spouse soon became apparent. Today, in virtually all jurisdictions, inter-spousal immunity has been abolished. Married persons owe their spouses the same general duty of reasonable care under all the circumstances as is owed to the rest of the world.

The vast majority of states have also abolished parent-child immunity, but in this case, a few still retain a no-duty approach for certain specific situations. For instance, the Wisconsin Supreme Court has held that a parent cannot be held liable for decisions relating to the exercise of parental authority over a child or those involving discretionary decisions about the provision of food, clothing, housing, or medical care. Under this approach, a child struck by the family car as dad is backing out of the driveway would have a valid claim if dad did not drive reasonably. However, the child would not have a claim if a parent unreasonably decided that complaints of a tummy ache did not warrant a trip to the doctor, even though the delay in securing medical care causes injury to the child. Other states, such as California, have found these exceptions too hard to administer and simply hold parents to a "reasonable parent" standard of care.

A somewhat similar historical evolution of the law can be found in negligence claims against charitable organizations. Originally they were held to be completely immune from suit, meaning that they owed no duty of care to the rest of us. To some extent, this reflected a notion that because they were acting in the public good, their carelessness should be excused. It also was based on a concern that requiring them to pay tort judgments might bankrupt them and deprive the community of their services. Whatever the rationale, the rule operated to deny recovery both to beneficiaries of the charity—such as patients at a charitable hospital—and to strangers, such as the pedestrian run down by a charity's negligently driven truck.

As insurance became more widely available, however, the rule of charitable immunity began to seem illogical, and today non-profit and charitable groups are liable for negligence in most jurisdictions. A remnant of the immunity remains in a number of states however, where liability is capped at a certain dollar amount, or where a charity cannot be held liable for more than the amount of any insurance that they have purchased.

CHAPTER IV

Negligence: The Breach Element

1. The Two Aspects of Proving Breach of Duty

The breach element of a negligence case obligates the plaintiff to demonstrate how, specifically, the defendant fell short of the legally required duty of care. There are two aspects of making such a showing. First, the plaintiff must identify some specific wrongful conduct—either an act or an omission—and convince the jury that this conduct did, in fact, take place. For instance, a plaintiff who was hit by a car might argue that the wrongful or faulty conduct was that the defendant was talking on a cell phone just seconds before impact. In some cases—indeed in most of the cases that wind up going to a trial—the defendant might deny that he was engaged in the alleged conduct. The evidence on this disputed point might, in my example, include cell phone records, the testimony of any eyewitnesses, and the testimony and cross-examination of the defendant himself. It is up to the jury to determine *what happened*.

But it is not enough for the plaintiff to identify and prove wrongful conduct. The second part of the breach element is to persuade the jury that the conduct falls below the standard of care. The defendant might concede that he was talking on his phone, but argue that he did not take his eyes off the road, and that it is not unreasonable to talk on the phone while driving. The plaintiff must show that reasonable people do not, and should not, use cell phones while driving. It is up to the jury to *evaluate* what happened and determine if it falls short of the care required by law.

2. The Relationship Between Duty and Breach

The "evaluation" aspect of the breach element involves a comparison between the alleged faulty conduct of the defendant and the relevant legal standard of care. You no doubt recall that there are quite a large number of possible duty rules depending on the kind of case plaintiff is litigating. A key point to bear in mind is that the *more specific* the duty, the less significant this evaluation process will be.

Let us compare two situations to illustrate this point. In case one we have a pedestrian who is struck by a car as he is crossing the street. Alleging that the driver ran a red light, the plaintiff convinces the court to use the "stop at a red light" statute as a duty of care. This is a very specific standard of care. Plaintiff then offers evidence of the allegedly faulty conduct, namely that the defendant ran the red light. For instance, plaintiff calls two eyewitnesses, each of whom testify that the light was red when defendant entered the intersection. If the jury believes that evidence, what "evaluation" must they conduct to determine if there was a breach? The answer is basically none. Since the duty is "don't run the light" and since the jury has found that defendant did run the light, that would be the end of the matter—breach established. Indeed, that is why the violation of a statutory standard of care is called "negligence per se." Because the duty is very specific the evaluation function of the jury largely disappears.

In our second case let us assume a pedestrian is hit by a car on a country road. This time he alleges that the faulty conduct of the defendant was looking away from the road to glance at his infant in a car seat in the back of the vehicle. In this case, the duty of care would be the default standard of "reasonable care under all the circumstances," or the care of a "reasonably prudent person acting under similar circumstances." Even if the plaintiff conclusively proves that the defendant did indeed look away from the road, the jury will still have to determine whether they think that was unreasonable under the circumstances. Was it just a short glance? Was the baby crying? What was the driver's speed at the time he looked at the child? Was the road curvy or straight? All these things might factor into their evaluation. Because the standard is very general, the evaluation function of the jury looms large.

In cases like our second hypo, you might wonder what, if any, evidence the plaintiff can offer to guide the jury in its evaluation function. Traditionally, there have been three principal ways that the reasonableness of alleged faulty conduct can be assessed. Let us consider them each in turn.

3. Assessing Reasonableness By Considering Custom

"Custom" is any practice followed by all or most people when engaging in a certain activity. Particularly in industrial contexts, there may often be customary ways of doing a task. It may be customary, for instance, to turn off the power switch of a certain machine used in a factory when walking away from it. A plaintiff can point to custom to argue that it sheds light on what would have been reasonable under the circumstances. The plaintiff will do this, of course, when the defendant departed from the custom. The argument is "most people turn off the switch, but you didn't turn off the switch, so that tends to show that you did not act reasonably."

This kind of evidence and argument is always admissible on the breach issue, but it is never conclusive. The defendant can always argue that there were good reasons for departing from custom on this particular occasion. Defendant can also claim that the custom has nothing to do with safety—for instance that people turn off the switch to save money on electricity, not to prevent accidents. Indeed, the defendant can claim that there really isn't a custom at all—that some workers in some factories do turn off the switch, but others do not.

Sometimes the defendant may be the one to invoke custom. The defendant may argue that no one, or virtually no one, takes the precaution that plaintiff says should have been taken. Since the defendant's conduct conforms to the norm, the defendant argues that he was reasonable under the circumstances. We can think of this as using custom evidence as shield instead of as a sword. Just flip the earlier hypo around for an example. Assume that the custom in the industry is to leave the machine running when walking away from it. Plaintiff has alleged that the failure to turn off the machine was a breach—unreasonable under the circumstances. The defendant would point to the custom to argue that since no one turns off the machine when walking away from it, it was reasonable for defendant to leave it running when he walked away.

The defendant in the famous case of *The T.J. Hooper* made this kind of argument. In that case, a tug boat got caught in stormy weather and the cargo it was towing was lost at sea. The cargo owner alleged that defendant's breach was its failure to have a radio on board, which would have been useful in getting weather reports. Defendant offered evidence that none (or very few) of the other tug boats had radios. Judge Learned Hand upheld findings that the defendant had been unreasonable despite the custom evidence. As he put it, in his typically learned fashion, a "whole calling" may have "lagged" in adopting new safety devices. Why Judge Hand thought he knew better than the entire tug boat industry is hard to say. Perhaps it was because his hand was so learned?

Closely related to custom evidence is evidence of industry standards. In some industries, various organizations may have promulgated model codes or other sets of rules recommending how various tasks should be performed. Assuming that these materials come from an organization with some expertise or credibility, they can also be offered in evidence to suggest how a reasonable person should have behaved.

4. Assessing Reasonableness By Considering Costs and Benefits

Reasonable people, supposedly, would be willing to spend a small amount of money or exert a small amount of effort in order to avoid a big harm. On the other hand, reasonable people do not normally spend large amounts of money or exert a great deal of effort to avoid a small or highly unlikely harm. This amounts to nothing more than saying that reasonable people consider the costs and benefits of their actions. It is, among other things, a very popular way to think about "reasonableness" among those who are economically oriented.

The most iconic statement of this notion about how to assess or evaluate reasonableness is the so-called *Carroll Towing* formula, articulated by Judge Learned Hand in the case of that name. In that case he declared that a reasonable person takes a precaution when $B < P \times L$, where B is the burden (or cost) of taking that precaution, where P is the probability that an injury will occur without the precaution, and where L is the magnitude of the injury, or loss.

Because the Hand or *Carroll Towing* formula is rendered as a mathematical equation, it tends to freak out math-phobic law students. An example may serve to make it more concrete. Assume that a customer at a store is mugged on the parking lot. The customer sues the store, alleging that they owed a duty to exercise reasonable care to protect her from a third-party source of harm (the mugger) since she was an invitee on their property. To show a breach of this duty she alleges that they should have had better lighting in the parking lot. How does she use the Hand formula to demonstrate that a reasonable store would have invested in the lighting?

Assume that the better lighting would have cost $500. Assume that a survey of other stores reveals that there is a 1% chance of a mugging over the course of a year at stores with lighted parking lots and a 3% chance at stores without lights. Finally, assume that the average mugging inflicts $30,000 in harm (which would include the medical bills and lost wages of victims, any property stolen, and the pain and fear suffered by the victims). The mugging rates reveal that the *increased probability* of a mugging without the precaution (the lights) is 2%. Multiplying that figure times the loss associated with a mugging yields $600 (in other words 2% of 30,000—if you can't do the math, use your calculator and multiply 30,000 x .02). To prevent that loss would have required spending $500 on lights. Since $500 is less than

$600, B is less than P x L, and a reasonable person would have spent the money on the lights. This means that the store committed a breach of duty by failing to put in lights.

You may be inclined to point out that lights presumably could last for more than one year, but our mugging statistics were yearly numbers. That is an excellent point. The numbers involved must both be based on the same time period. We can clarify the previous example, therefore, by saying that lights would actually cost $10,000, but that they would last for 20 years, giving us an annual cost of $500 a year. You would also be correct to note that the cost of lights includes not just installation, but also maintenance and electricity. Accurate analysis under the Hand formula should take these numbers into account as well.

Another aspect of the Hand formula may be puzzling. In our example it is the *store owner* who has to spend the money on the lights, but the costs of any mugging injuries are not really his costs—they are suffered by the *customers.* You might argue that a rational (or reasonable) person would never spend money on lights because whatever may happen on the dark parking lot is not his problem. The whole point of the Hand formula, however, is to make it his problem—to impose liability if a person who would directly suffer the harm would have spent the money on safety. This reflects a moral judgment that each of us should protect others when we would protect ourselves. You already learned this principle. In Sunday School. It's called the Golden Rule.

The Hand formula is usually not applied explicitly in the actual trial of negligence cases. Rather, it is a guideline that directs the lawyers to relevant evidence and helps them formulate persuasive arguments. In our example, it is unlikely that precise data could be found on the percentage by which better lighting will reduce muggings. Nonetheless, thinking about the Hand formula might inspire a plaintiff's lawyer to call an expert witness who could testify generally about how lights reduce crime. It also might inspire the plaintiff's lawyer to offer evidence about how inexpensive it would have been to install the lights.

In cases where the alleged breach is a momentary lapse in attention, or a faulty reaction in the heat of the moment, the Hand formula does not work very well. If, in an auto accident, the alleged breach is that the driver of the car took his eyes off the road to glance at his baby in the back seat, there really is no way to put a dollar value on the "burden" of keeping one's eyes constantly on the road. Most juries would not think about the case in terms of dollars and cents, and most appellate courts would not invoke cost-benefit analysis in their review of the verdict.

Note that reliance on the Hand formula and reliance on custom evidence are not mutually exclusive. A plaintiff can show that the failure to put lights in a parking lot was unreasonable because (1) lights are cheap and stop lots of crimes, and (2) most of the other stores have lights. The combination would be a powerful way to show that a reasonably prudent store would have installed lights. Note also that custom can be, in a sense, just a rough version of the Hand formula in action. After all, if everyone takes a precaution, that precaution is likely to be relatively inexpensive, the risks of harm without it are probably relatively great, and the amount of harm that could occur without the precaution is presumably significant.

5. Assessing Reasonableness By Appealing to Jury Intuition

In many cases the assessment of reasonableness is simply left to the jury's common sense and experience. Once they resolve any factual disputes and determine how the defendant behaved, they use their intuition to decide if that behavior was excessively risky, or whether the defendant acted reasonably. This allows the negligence system to reflect community values and to take into account all the myriad subtle differences in the facts that can lead to an accident. It also means, however, that the cases can be wildly inconsistent since different juries may come to different conclusions about the breach question in cases with very similar facts.

Plaintiffs in cases of this type sometimes argue to the jury that the risk of an injury like the one which occurred was highly foreseeable under the circumstances, and therefore that a reasonable person would have been more careful than the defendant. One might expect to hear this kind of argument in a case where defendant was driving home at 45 miles an hour on a snowy evening, the plaintiff's point being that defendant should have been driving more slowly. This is merely a soft form of arguing about the "P" term in Hand's famous formula—it is a claim that because the probability of harm was very high, absent the precaution of slower driving, a failure to take that precaution should be considered unreasonable.

Another common argument in these more intuitive kinds of cases is the defendant's claim that the plaintiff was capable of protecting himself from harm. The defendant's point is that if plaintiff could protect himself, it was not unreasonable for the defendant to omit additional precautions. In one federal case from Illinois, a truck driver was in a field to pick up a load of corn that was being discharged from a harvesting machine. The machine in question was apparently very large and made very loud noises when it was operating. The truck driver was so captivated by the spectacle of corn streaming into the bed of his truck that he stepped into the still moving harvesting blades and sustained quite terrible injuries. He alleged that the man operating the harvester was negligent in not turning off the machine. The trial court directed a verdict for the defendant and the appellate court affirmed. They reasoned that the danger was so obvious, given the visibility and noise of the machine, that the defendant was reasonable in assuming that plaintiff would simply avoid the danger. That meant that there was no breach of duty by the operator in failing to turn off the machine. Again, this is a casual argument about the "P" term in Hand's formula, this time claiming that the risk of harm was quite low, because the plaintiff could have protected himself.

Academic writers and law professors who teach torts do not spend a lot of time on the idea of reasonableness as an appeal to jury intuition. That is because there is not much to say about it. It is sort of a "know it when you see it" kind of approach. In the real world of personal injury litigation, however, it is quite common. This is one reason why law professors and personal injury lawyers rarely go drinking together.

6. Res Ipsa Loquitur

Sometimes the plaintiff lacks information about just what faulty conduct the defendant might have committed to cause the accident. In other words, the defendant does not have evidence of a specific breach of duty. A common modern example might be an airplane crash where all aboard are killed. It may be impossible to tell whether the pilot made an error in operating the plane and what specific error that might have been, or whether the pilot was drunk before starting the flight, or whether the plane had been negligently maintained, or whether the plane ran out of gas.

Normally, a plaintiff in this kind of case is out of luck. Without specific evidence on the breach element of the claim his case should be dismissed. However, in an act of judicial generosity, the courts have developed a doctrine that gives such a plaintiff an alternative way to go forward. The doctrine is known to this day by its Latin name—*res ipsa loquitur*—which means, roughly, "the thing speaks for itself." The notion is that some accidents are so often the product of careless behavior that we can assume that some sort of careless behavior must have been involved in this particular instance even though we don't know exactly what it was.

To invoke the doctrine, a plaintiff must make a two-prong showing. First, plaintiff must demonstrate that the accident is one normally associated with negligence. The word "normally" here is essentially a reference to probability. It means that this kind of accident usually, typically or more often than not, is due to carelessness of some kind. Second, plaintiff must show that it was the defendant who most probably was the careless party. A plaintiff who can satisfy these two tests will get to the jury despite the lack of concrete proof of a breach. As the leading Hornbook on Torts puts it, "the circumstances warrant the belief that the defendant was negligent in a wholly mysterious way."[1]

For a great many cases, the first prong of the res ipsa "showing" is nothing more than an appeal to the jury's experience, knowledge, and common sense. In the current state of aviation, properly maintained and piloted planes rarely crash. When there is a crash, therefore, it is obviously more probable that there was some kind of negligence by the airline or its pilot than that some non-negligent event like sudden air turbulence brought down the plane. The jury knows that, and thus the plaintiff really need only prove the facts surrounding the accident to satisfy this aspect of the *res ipsa* test.

---

1 Dan B. Dobbs, *The Law of Torts* (2000) 372.

Of course, not every accident by itself suggests probable negligence of the defendant. If a supermarket customer slips on some liquid on the floor and proves nothing further, that would not be enough to invoke *res ipsa* and get the case to the jury. After all, the store would only have been unreasonable if an employee was the one who spilled the liquid, or if the liquid had been on the floor for such a long time that a reasonable store would have known about it and cleaned it up. However, it is equally probable, isn't it, that a customer spilled the liquid and did so only a few minutes before the plaintiff slipped. Such a plaintiff could only succeed, therefore, if he offered some evidence of a specific breach, such as the testimony of a store clerk admitting that he was the one who carelessly spilled the liquid.

In some cases, the jury may lack experience and knowledge about the kind of accident which occurred. In these cases a plaintiff may offer expert testimony about probabilities to satisfy the requirements of the first part of the *res ipsa* doctrine. This is often the case in medical malpractice litigation. Let us assume that a plaintiff undergoes cosmetic surgery on his nose and emerges blind in one eye. More attractive now than before, but looking a bit like a pirate in his new rakish eye patch, the plaintiff sues the doctor. The plaintiff, of course, does not know what, if anything the surgeon might have done wrong during the operation, and the jury does not know if blindness is a potential complication of a nose job that is done non-negligently. In this case, the plaintiff can call a medical expert to testify that blindness never (or almost never) happens unless the surgery was done carelessly, in order to make out the first part of the *res ipsa* showing. We still don't know exactly what the negligent act might have been, but now there is a basis to say that some kind of carelessness is more probable than not.

The second prong of the *res ipsa* test —that any breach which took place was probably the responsibility of defendant—is usually established by showing that defendant had control over the object that caused the injury, or had custody over the plaintiff at the time of the injury. If plaintiff was hit by, oh let us say a wooden barrel, that fell from defendant's second story window, it is pretty clear that any negligent act would have been defendant's act, because defendant was in control of the barrel. Some courts, and some texts, list as a further requirement for *res ipsa* that the plaintiff demonstrate that he did not cause his own injury. This, of course, is really just another way of saying that plaintiff must prove that the defendant was mostly likely the negligent party, because ruling out his own negligence points the accusing finger exclusively at the defendant.

In some cases, particularly in the medical context, the plaintiff cannot show which of several defendants is the probable perpetrator of any negligent act. For instance, assume that after surgery on your arm, you awaken with third degree burns on your buttocks. Something clearly went wrong during this operation. The problem is that there were several people in the room at the time—the surgeon, the anesthesiologist, some nurses, and perhaps a medical student as well. You cannot say which of them most probably burned your posterior because you were under anesthesia. In this situation, a number of cases allow the injured party to use *res ipsa* against all the defendants as a group. Of course, if any individual defendant can convince the jury that he or she was not responsible, that defendant will be exonerated. The others, however, would be held jointly liable.

What happens once a plaintiff successfully invokes the *res ipsa* doctrine? In most states, the plaintiff is allowed to get to the jury, but *res ipsa* does not guarantee the plaintiff a verdict in his favor. The jury remains free to reject the inference of breach and find for the defendant. In a minority of states, *res ipsa* has a more potent procedural effect; it imposes an obligation on the defendant to offer some rebuttal evidence suggesting that he was not negligent. In these states, the failure of the defendant to respond would result in a verdict in plaintiff's favor. Technically speaking, the majority rule treats *res ipsa* as a "mere inference" while the minority position treats it as "presumption." You will learn more—perhaps more than you would like—about these notions if you opt to take a course on evidence.

CHAPTER V

Negligence: Factual Causation

1. The Basic Test—The "But-For" Rule

Having shown a breach, a plaintiff is next obligated to demonstrate a connection or linkage between that breach and the harm that he has suffered. If there is no such linkage, there is no moral or logical justification in forcing a defendant to pay damages. If I run a red light and hit you as you are crossing the street, and the next day you are diagnosed with lung cancer, it would only make sense to allow you to recover damages for cancer if my breach was in some way the cause of the cancer. If you would have gotten cancer anyway, my breach—as morally despicable as it may be—does not provide a justification for forcing me to compensate you.

The traditional test of factual causation is known as the "but-for" test. As the name suggestions, it requires us to speculate on whether—but for defendant's breach—the plaintiff would be uninjured. Essentially the jury is asked to imagine a hypothetical parallel universe in which everything happened the same way *except* that in this universe the defendant behaved with the legally required reasonable care. If in this parallel universe the plaintiff still gets hurt, that demonstrates the defendant's breach didn't make any difference. It's not crucial to the story, and it is thus not a factual cause. On the other hand, if the plaintiff would avoid injury in that parallel universe, that will establish causation under the but-for test.

Assume that Percy decides to go deep sea fishing on a ship operated by Dameon. During the excursion there is a violent storm and a huge wave washes Percy overboard, whereupon he is immediately sucked under the surface by a strong undertow. Percy is dead. His family sues Dameon. Their investigation reveals that his ship lacked donut-ring style life preservers. Consequently, in their negligence suit they allege that a statutory duty of care existed in this case, because a federal law requires ships to have a specified number of the donut-rings. Because Dameon violated the statute, Percy's family would be able to show negligence (breach) per se. The question remains, however, whether the breach was the cause of Percy's demise.

Let us imagine our parallel universe. In that situation, Dameon has the donut-rings, and throws one or more into the sea as soon as he realizes Percy's plight. Would that have made any difference? The answer is no, because the facts state that Percy was immediately caught up in the undertow. That means that he would not have been able to grab a donut-ring even if one had been thrown. Since Percy dies in the parallel universe just as he did in the real world, the breach really did not matter one way or the other—it is not a but-for cause. So in this case Dameon would not be liable.

Note that in making this kind of argument, the defendant uses the formula "even if." His argument is that "even if I had been reasonably prudent, you still would have suffered your injuries." Obviously, the parties are free to introduce any evidence they think might be relevant to this issue. In our Percy versus Dameon case, there might be testimony about whether any other passengers saw Dameon in the few minutes after he hit the water, about whether a donut-ring would have been sufficient to enable someone to resist an undertow, and about how strong a swimmer Percy was. At the end of the day, it would be up to jury to determine if life-rings would have made a difference, or if Percy was a dead man the minute he went overboard.

In certain situations, the factual cause issue can be difficult because of scientific ambiguity or long latency periods between the defendant's breach and the plaintiff's injury. For instance, if a defendant carelessly releases pollutants into the local water supply and someone develops cancer some years later, establishing that the pollutants caused the cancer could be difficult. The scientific link between that particular chemical and the particular cancer that the plaintiff suffers may be ambiguous, and plaintiff might have been genetically predisposed to cancer regardless of any exposure to hazardous chemicals. Cases of this sort call for expert testimony, and where that testimony is conflicting, the jury is obliged to sort it out. It is still, however, a matter of determining whether, more likely than not, "but for" the careless release of the chemicals, plaintiff would be healthy.

Events do not have a single factual or "but-for" cause. Indeed, events have an infinite number of causes. If Petunia is hit by a driver going 10 miles over the speed limit, among the multitude of causes for that event are the fact that Petunia decided to go out for a walk that day, the fact that the driver's car started that morning, the fact that both of them decided to live in the same city some years earlier, the fact that some urban planner decided to put a crosswalk at that location, and on and on. In some cases, therefore, we might have two defendants who commit completely different negligent acts, and each of them might be a but-for cause.

Assume that Dabny, an employee at a supermarket, negligently drops a glass bottle of juice on the floor. In attempting to pick up the bits of glass he cuts himself and so leaves the area to bandage his wound. Driscoll, the store manager, heard the noise of the breaking bottle, but was preoccupied by a fight he had just had with his wife on the phone and so forgets to clean up the spill. Ten minutes later Petunia slips on the juice and injures herself. The negligent acts of both Dabny and Driscoll are "but-for" causes of Petunia's injuries. If Dabny had been more careful and not dropped the bottle, Petunia would not have been hurt. If Driscoll had been more focused on his job, he would have cleaned the spill promptly and Petunia would not have been hurt. In a case like this the traditional rule is that the defendants would be jointly liable to Petunia. (As we will see a bit further on, many states now would assign each defendant a percentage of the blame, and they would each only be liable for that percentage of Petunia's damages).

While the "but-for" approach works well in most cases, it can lead to curious results in some situations, especially those involving multiple defendants. The next two sections consider the two most common special cases.

2. The Special Situation of Merged Causes

Imagine that two individuals who have no connection to each other both commit a negligent act (a breach of duty), and that their breaches each cause some kind of destructive force to be released.

A common, almost iconic, example would be if Al and Bill both negligently started fires that began burning in separate areas of a forest. Now further imagine that the two fires combine or merge together into a single conflagration which then destroys the plaintiff's house. In this kind of case, an attempt to use the but-for approach would lead to an odd result. Let us consider why.

Under a but-for analysis, Al could claim that "even if" he had been reasonably prudent, and never started a fire, the plaintiff's house would still have been destroyed by Bill's fire. If that claim is valid then it really didn't make a difference whether Al was careful or careless and his breach of duty is not a but-for cause of the plaintiff's harm. The problem is that Bill could make the exact same claim—arguing that even if he had been a veritable Smokey the Bear, Al's fire would have burned the plaintiff's property. Because there are two negligent parties and because their negligence merged, neither breach was essential to the harm. Neither party, in other words, was a but-for cause.

But that would lead to a silly result—namely that the plaintiff, who was entirely free from blame, could not recover against either careless fire-starter. To avoid that silly result, courts use an alternative test in cases such as this, known as the "substantial factor" approach. Each defendant is deemed a factual cause if his breach was a *substantial* factor in producing plaintiff's harm. A substantial factor is defined as a breach that could have caused the injury in question all by itself if there had been no other negligent acts involved in the scenario. In our simple example, since either fire could have destroyed the house by itself, both are substantial factors.

Not all merged cause situations require the use of the substantial factor test. In some cases, neither cause alone could have caused the harm, but together they are sufficient to do damage. In that kind of fact-pattern, because both are necessary to do the harm, both are but-for causes. Here is how that might occur. Assume Alpha Corporation and Beta Industries both negligently discharge 100 units of a chemical we will call salmonkilla from their respective factories. The salmonkilla from both companies flows into plaintiff's pond killing all his, you guessed it, salmon. Evidence at trial reveals that it takes 150 units of salmonkilla to kill a salmon. This means that neither breach, if it had happened alone, would have been sufficient to cause harm—neither, in other words is a substantial factor. Both breaches, however, are but-for causes, because if Alpha had been careful, the plaintiff's fish would be alive today, and if Beta had been careful, same thing. Thus, both defendants are liable.

3. Unascertainable Causes

In some cases involving multiple defendants, it will be clear that all of them committed a breach. However, it will be equally clear that only one of those breaches produced the harm suffered by the plaintiff; the others did not contribute to the harm in any way. However, we will not be able to determine *which* breach produced the harm. We can call this the problem of "unascertainable cause."

The classic case illustrating the problem is the California decision of *Summers v. Tice.* In that case three men were out quail hunting. Summers had separated from his colleagues and was off doing his own thing some distance away. The other two found some quail and fired their shotguns simultaneously, hoping to down one of the birds. Unfortunately, notwithstanding that they had an unobstructed view of Summers and knew where he was standing, they were so wildly enthusiastic to kill the poor bird that they fired in Summers' direction. One single shotgun pellet hit Summers in the eye. So now blind in one eye, Summers sued the other two.

The problem in this case was that plaintiff could not prove by a preponderance of the evidence that the breach of either defendant factually caused his injury. Since he had only been hit by one pellet, it is clear that only one breach was the cause of harm, and that the other breach caused nothing. One of the two negligent acts literally went harmlessly into the sky. Unfortunately, there was no way to know which was which because the two defendants acted at the same exact moment and were standing in the exact same location. The most that we can say is that there is a 50% chance the harmful pellet came from defendant A and a 50% chance that it came from defendant B. Since a "preponderance" of the evidence requires proof greater than 50%, plaintiff appears to be the victim of a dilemma in a case like this.

To solve the dilemma, the California Supreme Court held that, in this kind of situation, it would shift the burden of proof. The defendants would have the obligation to come forward with evidence showing that their breach did not put out the plaintiff's eye. If one of the defendants could succeed in carrying this burden, that defendant would be exonerated and the other defendant would be stuck paying all the damages. Otherwise, the two defendants would be jointly and severally liable.

A modern variation on the *Summers v. Tice* situation arises when several firms sell the same product which, after a long delay, is discovered to have harmful properties. Assume that Payton took a medication during her pregnancy to control morning sickness. Ten years later Payton develops an illness that is directly traceable to that medication. There were four different companies that made and sold the medication back when she was pregnant but now that a decade has passed, she has no idea which of the four supplied the product that she consumed. Only one of the companies (let us call them Alpha, Beta, Gamma, and Delta) is the factual cause of her harm, but neither she nor anyone else can ascertain which one. Just like *Summers*, factual causation is unascertainable here. It is as if all four companies fired a pill at Payton and she was hit by only one, but we don't know which one.

Under the rule in *Summers* the companies will bear the burden of demonstrating that their sales could *not* have been the ones that affected Payton. If none of the defendants can satisfy this burden, most modern decisions hold them liable in proportion to their market share for the drug in question. In other words, if Alpha made 40% of the total sales, it would owe Payton 40% of her total damages. Similarly with the other defendants.

4. The "Loss of Chance" Cases

Assume that Parnell has contracted a very serious disease (unrelated to either his own or anyone else's negligence), which we will call "tryptonosis" (I am making this name up). Even with state of the art medical treatment, the likelihood that someone with tryptonosis will survive the ailment is only 40%. In other words, there is a 60% chance of death from the illness under the best of circumstances. Parnell consults Dr. Dante. Alas, Dr. Dante makes an error in treating Parnell—perhaps he gives him the wrong medication for his tryptonosis or perhaps he misses the diagnosis entirely and tells Parnell, "it's just a headache—you'll be fine in a day or two." Within a matter of weeks Parnell is dead, and his family brings a malpractice suit against Dante.

Do you see a factual causation problem here? If not, apply the but-for test of causation that we covered at the start of the chapter and see what happens. Can we say that but for Dante's error, Parnell would be alive today? Actually not. If Dante had done everything correctly it is still more likely than not that Parnell would be dead, because even properly treated tryptonosis sufferers die more often than not (60% of the time to be precise). Given the statistics, it would seem that Parnell was probably going to die no matter what Dante did. Consequently, his family's suit should be dismissed.

Of course, that result has a few problems. First, it doesn't exactly provide incentives to doctors to use their best efforts to treat tryptonosis. It would mean that when people with serious illnesses that are hard to cure show up at the doctor's office there would be no reason for doctors to be careful or use state of the art medical technology. Not only that, but denying relief doesn't correspond with the natural human desire to receive the greatest possible chance for a recovery, even if that chance is less than 50-50. If you had a 4 out of 10 chance to survive I am sure you would want your doctor to exert his or her best efforts to maximize your chances.

Given these and other concerns, a number of states have decided to relax the usual rules of factual causation in situations like our hypothetical. Under what has become known as the "loss of chance" rule, plaintiffs like Parnell's family are allowed to recover the value of the chance for a cure that the doctor negligently destroyed or eliminated. As the Missouri Supreme Court put it in one case, "A patient with cancer . . . would pay to have a choice between three unmarked doors—behind two of which were death, with life the third option. A physician who deprived a patient of this opportunity, even though only a one-third chance, would have caused her real harm." The value of the chance is usually a percentage of the total damages proven equal to the percentage chance for recovery that the plaintiff would have had if the doctor had exercised appropriate care. Thus, if the Parnell family proved $1,000,000 in damages due to his death, they would recover $400,000 under the loss of chance theory.

Not all courts recognize the loss of chance theory, though the number that do has increased in recent years. You should be aware that some courts still adhere to the strict rule of but-for causation and deny relief in cases of this sort. As with all things "tort," the moral of the story is that you need to research the law in your own jurisdiction before making representations to a client or a court.

CHAPTER VI

Negligence: Proximate Cause

1. An Introduction

Proximate cause is often said to be the most conceptually difficult of all the elements of the negligence tort. If there is any basis for this reputation, my own view is that it is because of the label "proximate cause." That could be one of the most unhelpful designations for a legal principle in the history of jurisprudence. Let us see if we can put the label aside and just make a few general comments.

Every act that each of commits can change, in some small way, the entire future course of events. To be more poetic about it—every event has "ripple effects" that will continue until the end of time. This is especially true when the act in question is an injury-producing act that is the product of negligence. If you run a red light and kill a pedestrian, that individual might have been a research scientist working on a cure for cancer. His death might set the research back by years, and thus some number of other persons who might have lived longer lives will die prematurely of their cancers. Some of those individuals, in turn, might have become senior diplomats, if only they had lived, and in that capacity might have prevented a future war. The thousands who die in that subsequent war would not have died if you had not run the red light. You are a "but for" cause of all of those deaths.

Despite the fact that you are one cause (of an infinite number of causes) that led to all those war deaths, it just doesn't seem logical, or even fair, to hold you legally responsible to pay damages to all those war widows and their children. Intuition tells us there has to be some end point to your legal responsibility. Without such an end point, the legal risks of acting in any fashion would be so daunting that most of us would just stay home and hide under the covers.

The proximate cause element of negligence is an effort to delineate the outer limit of liability. Phrased as an element of plaintiff's case, it requires a plaintiff to convince the court that his injury has a sufficiently close connection to the defendant's breach that liability *would be fair under the circumstances*. It's sort of an "eleventh-hour" sanity check, late in the case for negligence, that requires plaintiff to show that liability makes sense.

The newest version of the Restatement of Torts—the Third Restatement—abandons the use of the phrase "proximate cause" and substitutes the label "scope of responsibility." (Actually, they do invoke the words "proximate cause" in a parentheses.) This is a commendable effort to use a more accurate label to describe what this element of the case is really about. The element obligates the plaintiff to show that his injuries are within the scope of appropriate liability or responsibility for this particular defendant.

I fear, however, that the authors of the Third Restatement are unduly optimistic in thinking that their new terminology will catch on. The proximate cause label has been around for nearly a century. It is likely to remain around for a long time to come—certainly it will be around when you take your Torts exam, and so you are likely stuck with it for the time being. For the rest of this chapter, I will alternate between referring to the element by the traditional label ("proximate cause"), my label ("fairness") and the Restatement label ("scope of responsibility"). This is not an attempt to drive you crazy. Rather, by using all three designations, I hope that you will get a more intuitive sense of what this element is really about by the time we finish the chapter.

As theoretically interesting as the problem of infinite liability might be, the good news is that in most cases, it's not a practical problem. Plaintiffs tend to sue obvious defendants first, at least when they have money (or insurance, which is the same thing). When the defendant is obvious—someone whose carelessness is intimately and directly connected to the injury—the fairness of imposing liability seems self-evident. To put the same point another way, the connection between the defendant's breach and the plaintiff's harm in the typical negligence suit is so straightforward and so strong, and the fairness of making the defendant pay damages is so compelling, that there is no need to agonize over "proximate cause."

For instance, when a driver runs a red light, hits a pedestrian, and breaks his leg, it is obvious that the broken leg is within the driver's scope of responsibility. It is clearly fair to make him pay for it and there is no need to agonize over "proximate cause." It's not like the plaintiff is reaching back generations into the past to sue the doctor whose negligent sterilization procedure resulted in the driver's grandfather being born in the first place (because but for the botched sterilization the driver would never have been born and the pedestrian's leg would thus never have been broken). There is no issue about "cutting off" the driver's liability, because if the driver in a case of this sort is not liable, we would have essentially repealed the entire cause of action for negligence. Consequently, when you read opinions of this straightforward variety, you will discover that they simply do not include a discussion of the proximate cause element. Really. Go back and look at the cases in all the other chapters of your Torts casebook. You will discover that most make no mention of proximate cause at all because it is a non-issue on the facts presented. It is like a free-square on a Bingo card.

However, just because hard cases are rare, does not mean they are non-existent, and we have to have some method for dealing with them when they do eventually rear their ugly heads. Just bear in mind that while you may spend a lot of time on these kinds of problems in a torts course, because they are intellectually interesting (and fascinate your teacher), they tend to come up in only a small percentage of the cases that are actually litigated.

So on to the meat of the matter. How might the legal system specify a rule for "cutting off" the liability of a negligent defendant short of infinity, and limiting it to cases where liability would be fair? What, in other words, is the proper "scope of responsibility" of a careless defendant? Let us first consider a few really silly possibilities. They may help you see why the problem of designing a good rule has been a challenge for the legal system.

2. Really Silly Ideas For a Proximate Cause Test

It would be nice if we could use a "bright line" test in the proximate cause area. Such a test would be easy to administer—ideally it would be purely mechanical like a math formula. Unfortunately, those don't tend to make a great deal of practical sense, and no one has seriously proposed them.

For instance, we could have a rule that said that defendants are not liable for anything that happens more than 30 days after they commit a negligent act. That would be relatively easy to administer in most cases (though not in all, because sometimes we would have trouble pinning down when the negligent act took place). Such a rule would mean, however, that a company that negligently dumped toxic chemicals into a local water supply could escape all responsibility for illnesses that took more than 30 days to develop and a negligent surgeon would not be liable for consequences of malpractice that did not manifest themselves until weeks after an operation. While the passage of time does seem to have something to do with fixing the scope of responsibility and the fairness inquiry, a bright line test based on time would be arbitrary in the extreme and often might violate our notions of common sense or justice.

A rule based on distance instead of time would be equally silly. For instance, saying that a negligent party could only be liable for injuries that take place within 500 yards of his negligent act would mean that a doctor who negligently prescribed the wrong dose of a medication that caused a driver to black out would not be liable if the comatose driver hit a pedestrian a mile from the doctor's office. Once again, there is some logic to saying that distance from the defendant's acts may have some bearing on whether liability would be fair, but a bright-line rule based on some arbitrary distance would be absurd.

You might think that if we want to limit defendant's responsibility to reasonable bounds, the easiest way to do it would be to just put a dollar limit on that responsibility. For instance, adopt a rule that says "no defendant can be liable for more than $1,000,000 due to a single negligent act." That rule, however, does nothing to solve the real problem because it doesn't tell us *which victims* get a share of that money. In the you-ran-over-a-cancer-researcher hypo, does all the money go to the researcher's family? Do those who would have been cured of cancer but for the driver's carelessness get some of the money? And what about those war widows?

As these examples have, hopefully, made clear, the reason proximate cause has been a source of academic debate and some degree of law student agony is that designing a workable rule is tricky. Fortunately, you arrive at the study of negligence at a moment when there seems to be a relative consensus on how to tackle the problem. So, bravely onward to the next subsection where we will review the prevailing approach to the scope of responsibility problem.

3. Foreseeability As The Measure of Defendant's Liability

Most courts today take the view that a defendant should be liable for all *foreseeable consequences* of his negligent act that injure *foreseeable victims*, but nothing more. This idea is sometime called the "risk rule." The name alludes to the fact that a negligent act creates certain foreseeable risks, and when the resulting harm stems from one of those risks, the defendant is properly held liable.

The Restatement (Third) puts this very concisely in section 29: "An actor's liability is limited to those harms that result from the risks that made the actor's conduct tortious." A good illustration of how this limiting principle works are the facts of what is sometimes called the most famous torts case ever decided. That, of course, would be *Palsgraf v. Long Island R.R.* On the very remote chance that you have not read it, here is a brief summary of what happened.

Two men were seeking to board a railroad train that had already begun to slowly move out of a station. One of the men, who was holding a package, appeared about to lose his balance, so a nearby employee of the railroad gave him a push, thinking that this would help him into the railroad car. Unfortunately the push knocked the package out of his hands. The package was apparently loaded with powerful fireworks, which caused a major explosion in the station. One consequence of that explosion was injury to another passenger who was standing some distance away on the platform. Her name was Helen Palsgraf.

Helen sued the railroad for the allegedly negligent acts of its employee (the gentleman with the package apparently sped away on the train into legal obscurity and was never sued). The case wound up in the highest court of New York state. In a 4-3 decision Judge (later Supreme Court Justice and Law School) Benjamin Cardozo held that Helen could not recover.

The crux of Cardozo's view was that what happened to Helen was unforeseeable; indeed, that it was unforeseeable that anything would happen *to her* given the negligent act involved here. Recall that the negligent act, or breach, in the case was the clumsy push of the package-toting passenger by the railroad employee. What risks does that act entail? Well, certainly it entails the risk that the contents of the package could break. It might also entail a risk to the holder of the package, if the push was forceful enough, or alternatively if he bent to retrieve the package while the train was picking up speed. Perhaps it also even entails a risk to passengers standing next to the man with the package, because he might have lost his balance and fallen against them, causing them to injure themselves.

The risk of an explosion, however, was entirely unforeseeable. Who could have seen that coming? Similarly, any harm to Helen was entirely unpredictable because she was standing so far away. Because what happened was entirely different from what we expected—because it involved a result outside the foreseeable risk, to an unforeseeable victim—it is beyond the scope of the railroad's liability. It would be unfair to make them pay for it. They are thus not the "proximate cause" of Helen's harm.

Now before we go any further, I must hasten to add that Cardozo, while relying on foreseeability, did not actually frame his decision as relating to what we now call "proximate cause." Rather, he held that the railroad did not owe Helen any duty in the first place because she was outside what he called the "zone of danger." The author of the dissent—Judge Andrews—was the one who focused on "proximate cause" as the part of negligence law that would limit defendant's ultimate responsibility. However, Andrews' substantive test was more squishy than a pure foreseeability approach. He would have relied on a multi-factor test, which he candidly labeled "practical politics." Essentially what has happened is that most courts have adopted Cardozo's substantive test based on foreseeability, but not his approach of treating it as a matter of duty. Instead, foreseeability has become our test of fairness, scope of responsibility, or proximate cause.

4. An Obsolete Rule and Its Rhetorical Legacy

Just a few years before *Palsgraf* was decided, an English court confronted a case called *Polemis.* I am going to tell you a little bit about this case, but you need to understand that its holding or approach is no longer the law, even in England. I am not, however, wasting your time while I display my knowledge of British legal history. Although the substantive approach to scope of responsibility used by *Polemis* is now obsolete, the language of the opinion has influenced how courts talk about proximate cause.

In *Polemis* some workers were unloading a ship. On the deck was an open "hatch"—a big square opening to the cargo hold underneath the deck. On this particular ship the cargo included benzene, a flammable chemical with many uses. Because it was inefficient to walk around the hatch as they moved around the deck, the workers laid some planks over the hatch as sort of a footbridge. Of course one of them was clumsy and knocked one of the boards into the hold. It turned out that some of the benzene had vaporized, and when the plank fell, it created a spark that ignited the fumes and caused an explosion. (Not all proximate cause cases involve explosions, but since they tend to be surprising, they come up with some regularity in the proximate cause literature).

When the case was litigated the defendants argued that they shouldn't be liable because the accident which occurred was unforeseeable. The foreseeable risk, in their view, would have been injury to one of the workers down in the cargo hold who might have gotten hit on the head by the plank. Now, I suspect you don't know much about benzene, and neither do I. Let us take it as a given that no one would have expected the explosion; that it was as utterly shocking and unforeseeable as the blast that rocked the railroad station in *Palsgraf*. That would mean that defendant should not be liable. It would be unfair to hold them liable for something that was not a foreseeable aspect of the risk they created by knocking over the plank. It should be held to be outside their scope of responsibility. In the jargon, they are not the proximate cause of the explosion.

The English judges, however, saw it differently. They held that it did not matter whether the outcome was foreseeable in a case like this. Rather, they said that the defendant would be responsible for all the "direct" consequences of his actions. As one of the judges put it, "[t]he fire appears to me to have been directly caused by the falling of the plank. Under these circumstances I consider that it is immaterial that the causing of the spark by the falling of the plank could not have been reasonably anticipated."

Now, as noted at the start of this section, this is no longer the approach courts take to the issue of defendant's scope of liability. However, the use of the idea of "direct" cause spawned a rather messy vocabulary in some courts that persists to this day. Let us try to untangle the mess as quickly as we can.

The opposite of "direct" would, of course, be "indirect." An indirect cause situation might be one like this—Dirk is driving an open bed truck loaded with lumber, which he secured to the truck carelessly. As he is driving, a board falls off into the middle of the road. A few minutes later Ian comes driving down that same road at a negligent rate of speed. Seeing the board at the last minute, he has no time to brake, so he swerves abruptly, hitting Petunia, a pedestrian walking on the sidewalk. If Petunia sues Dirk, we certainly would not say that he caused her harm directly.

One might find in *Polemis* an implicit suggestion that a defendant should not be held liable for indirect consequences of a negligent act, but the case doesn't compel that result. Since *Polemis* involved a direct cause factual scenario, it just had no occasion to lay out rules for the indirect cause cases. Unfortunately, many subsequent cases decided that the best way to think about indirect cause cases was to focus on the event that happened in the middle of the story, which they began to call an "intervening cause." In my hypo, Ian's speeding would be an intervening cause (I named him Ian because starting his name with the letter "I" helps us keep in mind that he is the intervening cause in this case).

To make matters worse, courts then began to say that to resolve the proximate cause question in an intervening cause situation required a determination of whether the intervening cause was "superceding" (some said "supervening" which is the same thing). In this jargon, a "superceding" cause was one which "cut off" the responsibility of the actor whose liability was under discussion (Dirk, in our example).

Of course, all this required these courts to come up with rules about *when* an intervening cause should be considered superceding. In at least some cases, these rules became rather elaborate and, perhaps more regrettably, were often phrased in ponderous language that was very difficult to decipher and apply to concrete fact patterns.

The good news, however, is that the vast majority of these intervening-cause cases are really using the basic foreseeability test of scope of responsibility, no matter what their language. In the Petunia v. Dirk case, while some courts may spend several paragraphs discussing whether Ian's negligent driving was "superceding," at the end of the day, they decide the case based on whether what happened was part of the risk Dirk created when he negligently failed to secure the lumber in his truck. If it was within that risk then liability is fair, and it makes sense to call him a proximate cause of Petunia's injuries.

There is one particular type of intervening cause case that should never give you trouble. That would be the case where the defendant's duty is defined as preventing the intervening cause from doing harm in the first place! Think back to the duty chapter. There, we noted a class of cases where a duty is imposed on a party to protect others from a "third party source of harm." For instance, a school has a duty to take reasonable measures to protect its students from dangerous visitors or intruders in the school.

If the school fails to set up security procedures and a visitor assaults a student, what do you think of the following argument by the school's lawyer: "We can't be liable because the acts of the visitor are a 'superceding' cause that cuts off our liability. We had no reason to anticipate a criminal act by a third party." The argument is pretty ridiculous, isn't it? Since the school's duty was to protect students from dangerous visitors, it would be nonsensical to say that the violent act of one such visitor was the kind of surprise or unforeseeable outcome that would make this event something outside the scope of their responsibility. There is no reason to exonerate them on these facts; the very contingency that they were charged with protecting against has come to pass. In a case like this it would be appropriate to say, "where the duty requires defendant to protect against negligence or intentional harm by a third person, the acts of that third person are never a reason to deny relief on proximate cause grounds."

There are certain other intervening cause situations that are almost as straightforward. Cases in this group have been litigated so often that courts no longer engage in a case-by-case analysis. Rather, because they fit into well established patterns, the courts rely on past precedent. For instance, a large number of cases involve intervening medical negligence that makes an initial injury more severe. Assume that Dilbert negligently cut Pagano's leg when he dropped a glass bottle which shattered. Dilbert went to the hospital to have the wound treated, but the doctor committed malpractice by failing to sterilize his instruments and Pagano's leg wound was infected. Virtually all courts will hold Dilbert liable for the infection as well as for the initial wound.

The logic is that in some predictable percentage of cases doctors will make things worse rather than better. This is inevitable—some small percentage of doctors do make errors. When a medical error happens it is not the kind of shocking outcome that would make it unfair to hold the original negligent party responsible. Because it is fair to make Dilbert pay for the infection on these facts, courts conclude that it is within the scope of his responsibility and say that Dilbert was the proximate cause of the infection.

Another example of this type of case is one involving an intervening negligent rescue. In this case Dilbert again drops the glass bottle which cuts Pagano's leg. Dilbert then walks away leaving Pagano bleeding. Sam, a good Samaritan, arrives on the scene and, seeing Pagano, attempts to stop the bleeding. However, because he used a tourniquet that was too tight, the result is that Pagano's leg must be amputated. Here again, courts would hold that the amputation was within Dilbert's scope of responsibility—it is fair to make him pay for it and, in the traditional jargon he will be deemed the "proximate cause" of that amputation.

Still a third category where courts have enough experience to apply a settled rule involves cases where there is a second injury or accident to the original victim. For instance, if poor Pagano had his wound properly treated by a perfectly competent physician, but nonetheless developed an infection, the courts are clear that Dilbert would be responsible for that as well, since such an eventuality is entirely foreseeable, and foreseeability determines the scope of his responsibility.

Of course there are any number of situations involving a so-called "intervening" cause that will not fall into these patterns. The key to resolving them is to keep your eye firmly focused on the question of foreseeability. Ask yourself whether the misfortune that plaintiff suffered was the type of thing that could have been anticipated given the breach that the defendant committed. If so, then liability would seem fair—the intervening cause should not be labeled "superceding" and it should not "cut off" defendant's liability. On the other hand, if what happened to the poor plaintiff was a bit of a surprise, out of the ordinary, not what you expected given the breach, and a "I didn't see that coming" sort of outcome, you have the kind of case where plaintiff is likely to lose.

In one case from Georgia, a woman dining at a country club in Atlanta ordered a shrimp cocktail. Apparently the club, although exclusive, was not reasonably prudent. They had neglected to keep the shrimp refrigerated and it had gone bad. The unwitting guest soon felt ill and excused herself from the table. After a long interval, another woman—let's call her Patty—who had been dining with the shrimp-eater decided to check on her to see how she was doing. When Patty entered the lady's room, she saw her friend vomiting into a toilet bowl. Concerned for her friend's welfare, Patty did not notice a puddle of vomit on the bathroom floor. She slipped in that puddle and injured herself in the fall.

How would you analyze the "proximate cause" issue in the Patty versus country club lawsuit? It is, of course, an "intervening cause" kind of case. Shrimp-lady's unfortunate inability to make it to the toilet bowl before she began to hurl "intervened" between the country club's breach (serving bad shrimp) and the injury (Patty's broken bones). You could tie yourself in knots trying to determine if this particular intervening cause was "superceding," but it would be far easier to just ask whether what happened to Patty was foreseeable given the defendant's carelessness. In other words, what risks are associated with serving bad shrimp and were Patty's injury's within the scope of those risks?

The foreseeable risk associated with serving bad shrimp is food poisoning. In addition, there are further foreseeable risks that come along when doctors attempt to treat that food poisoning, such as contracting an infection at the hospital. But the chance that rotten shrimp will break the leg of someone who didn't even eat the shrimp is slim indeed. The way the whole story unfolded is a bit . . . unusual. Consequently, the court in the actual case denied recovery.[1]

5. Why It Gets Fuzzy: Characterizing the Risk

In order to determine whether the ultimate injury to plaintiff is foreseeable, and thus within defendant's scope of responsibility, it is necessary to identify the risks associated with defendant's breach. This is far from a mechanical process. Indeed, it is highly imprecise. That is why proximate cause decisions sometimes seem so murky. Let us expand on this a bit.

You might be tempted to say, in any given case, that the risk associated with defendant's breach is "injury to plaintiff." That wouldn't be a very good idea. If we did that, it would mean that *all* outcomes would be within the scope of defendant's responsibility no matter how bizarre or surprising or remote in time and space. Such an approach would effectively eliminate the fairness criterion and liability-limiting function that is at the heart of the proximate cause element. After all, the plaintiff is always injured—that is why we have a lawsuit. In *Palsgraf,* if the risk of shoving the man with the package was "injury to someone," then Helen Palsgraf's injury due to the surprise explosion of the concealed fireworks in the package would be within that risk—she was a someone and she got injured. In the shrimp case just considered, if the risk of serving bad shrimp is "injury to someone," then Patty's broken bones would similarly be within the risk.

1 This judicial monument to fine dining in Georgia is *Crankshaw v. Piedmont Driving Club*, 115 Ga. App. 820, 156 S.E.2d 208 (1967).

So, plaintiff cannot simply characterize the risk as "injury to someone" and leave it at that when considering the proximate cause element of a negligence case. Similarly, you cannot say that on a final exam. The plaintiff—and you—must be more precise, and identify a specific *type* of injury that might be the result of the breach, and a specific *class* of potential victims who might suffer because of the breach.

Just how precise the plaintiff must be, is, however, one of those things that the legal system has not defined. It is certainly not necessary that the accident unfold in a foreseeable fashion—only that the outcome be similar in nature to the kind of risks that might have been expected at the outset. For instance, in one New York case, a worker on a road construction crew was instructed to stand close to oncoming traffic with only a single wooden "sawhorse" style barrier protecting him. Some time later, a driver afflicted with epilepsy, who had neglected to take his medication on that fateful day, suffered a seizure, and drove through the barrier. The worker was propelled into the air and covered with super-heated liquid enamel in a caldron he had been attending. In the words of the court, he became a human fireball. He miraculously survived and as soon as he cooled down he filed a lawsuit.[2]

It is a fair bet that no one would have predicted that an unmedicated epileptic would run into the plaintiff and that the plaintiff would then be hurled up into the air and coated with scalding enamel. Even most law professors would have shied away from that scenario on a final exam as too preposterous. However, the breach in the case was forcing the man to stand near traffic in an unprotected, vulnerable position. The risk asso-

2 The facts are from *Derdiarian v. Felix Contracting Corp.*, 51 N.Y.2d 308 434 N.Y. Supp. 2d 166 (1980).

ciated with that breach is that he would get hit by a negligent driver (note that careful drivers would not hit him despite the flimsy barrier because they would be . . . careful). That is exactly the risk that materialized. While we might have expected a drunk driver, or a speeding driver, not an unmedicated epileptic driver, what happened is still within the general class of risks we should have expected.

Many courts, and many, many law professors have tried to come up with a theory that would help define the scope of risk associated with various breaches of duty. For the most part they have all failed, though most of the professors did get tenure. The problem is like trying to nail the proverbial jellyfish to a wall. The most that can be said while still keeping the conversation short and happy is that the extreme cases are easy, and the close cases go to the jury. That may sound like a cop out, but it has the virtue of being both accurate and concise.

CHAPTER VII

Negligence: Damages

1. Types of Damages Recoverable

Damages can either be "compensatory" or "punitive." As the labels suggest, the former are designed to compensate the plaintiff for the injuries suffered, and to restore him, as much as money can do so, to the position he enjoyed before he was victimized by the defendant's negligence. The latter, obviously, are meant to punish the defendant and thus to operate as a deterrent. Punitive damages are rarely awarded in negligence cases. Let us, however, defer further consideration of those and consider first the various elements that compose the typical compensatory award.

Most negligence plaintiffs are entitled to three types of compensatory damages. The first is for past and future medical expenses. While in many cases the calculation of medical expenses is straightforward, it can involve disputes where the injuries are severe and where the plaintiff may require an unknown number of future surgeries or an unknown amount of rehabilitation or nursing care over a period of many years. Litigants sometimes rely on expert testimony to estimate these costs but, as you would imagine, the experts for the two parties usually have wildly differing estimates.

The second traditional item of compensatory damages is lost wages. When the plaintiff is a middle-aged adult, well-settled on a career path, it is usually fairly easy to estimate what he would have earned during any period he is unable to work due to his injuries. Even in these cases, however, some guesswork is involved. Let us say that the plaintiff is a 38-year-old who has worked in the construction industry since graduating from high school. Let us say that he suffers a back injury as a result of an auto accident. It may be difficult to know for sure when, if at all, he will be able to return to work. It may be difficult to know if a recession would mean that he could only work part-time in the future. If his injuries make it impossible for him to resume construction work, we will have to predict what other, less physically demanding, work he might find and how much he would earn in that position. There is a lot of room for disagreement.

If the plaintiff is a younger person, and especially if the plaintiff is a child, the award of lost wages requires even more speculation. How are we to know whether an 8-year old who is left brain-damaged as a result of medical malpractice during a tonsillectomy would have grown up to become a high-earning CEO of a Fortune 500 corporation, or a customer-service operative in the exciting fast food industry? Courts rely on information about the economic status of members of the child's family, the child's expression of career interest, teachers' assessments of potential and other similar "tea leaves" to try to make a prediction. As you might imagine, much will turn on the persuasive skill of plaintiff's lawyer.

Both future medical expenses and lost wages are generally "discounted to present value." Since a lump sum of money received today can be invested and will, presumably, earn interest in the years before it is needed, the lump sum can be somewhat smaller than the sum of the periodic payments. In other words, if I want you to have $40,000 a year for the next 20 years, I don't need to give you $800,000. I can give you a lesser sum in light of the fact that you will be able to earn interest on some of that money for a decade or more. This principle is sometimes called the "time value of money." If you want to see how this works you can search online for "present value calculators" and plug in some numbers.

The final component of a compensatory damage award is compensation for "pain and suffering." These are often referred to as "non-economic" damages. This is an effort to compensate the plaintiff for the physical agony of the injury and the pain associated with any medical treatments, as well as for emotional consequences that flow from the injury. If the plaintiff has been paralyzed, the fact that he will no longer be able to dance with his wife, that he will need help going to the bathroom, and that he may not be able to have a normal sex life would all be taken into consideration by a jury in fixing the amount of damages. In cases where the plaintiff's injuries are severe, this item can often be many hundreds of thousands, or even several million, dollars.

Several state legislatures, in response to pleas from the business community and insurance companies, have adopted statutes capping pain-and-suffering awards. These caps vary a great deal not just numerically, but also in other details. Some only apply to certain types of cases, like medical malpractice. Some are inapplicable if the defendant was drunk. Some automatically go up each year to take into account changes in the cost of living, while other do not. Generalizations are perilous and you won't get them from me.

In addition to compensatory damages, tort victims are sometimes entitled to punitive damages, also known in some states as "exemplary" damages. This type of award is usually only made in cases involving intentional torts, or cases where the defendant has been reckless or engaged in other egregious conduct. Punitive damages are not usually available in cases of simple negligence. In some states, legislation provides that a portion of any punitive award is paid to the state, not to the plaintiff.

As the label suggests, the purpose of punitive damages is to punish the defendant. Ideally, they create a deterrent effect so that a defendant will not engage in the same tortious behavior in the future. Historically, there were few guidelines for the jury in setting a punitive award, and a few awards were truly jaw-dropping in amount. In recent years, the U.S. Supreme Court has held that the Constitution imposes limits on punitive damage awards and that excessive awards can violate "due process of law" because they operate like criminal penalties, but the defendant does not get the full protections of the criminal law in a civil tort suit.

While the Court did not claim to be laying down firm rules, it offered the guideline that punitive damages should not exceed a "single digit multiple" of compensatory damages, and in most cases should be no more than two or three times the compensatory award. The Supreme Court cases in question have largely involved corporate defendants—car manufacturers and insurance companies—and economic torts such as fraud or bad faith refusal to defend a law suit. Whether the same guidelines would be applied to a case where a defendant deliberately dumped highly toxic waste in a city water supply remains to be seen. It would be far too cynical—and political—to suggest that these decision may simply reflect a particular sympathy for corporations, so I certainly will not do that here.

2. The "Eggshell Skull" Principle

Innumerable cases have observed that a defendant "takes the plaintiff as he finds the plaintiff." What this means is that if the plaintiff is frail or weak, and suffers devastating injuries from an act that would have left a more robust individual hardly injured at all, the defendant must pay the plaintiff for all harm suffered. This rule is sometime also delightfully called the "eggshell skull rule."

In one case there was a minor auto accident that resulted in no physical injuries—a classic "fender bender." However, within minutes after the impact, a 14-year old girl riding in the car that had been struck "began to behave in a bizarre manner. After a series of hospitalizations, she was diagnosed as suffering from a schizophrenic reaction." Other evidence revealed that prior to the accident she suffered from what the court called a pre-psychotic personality. The appellate court held that if she could prove all this at trial, she would be entitled to recover for all her damages, even though the odds of developing schizophrenia from a minor car accident are remote, to say the least.

The eggshell skull rule is an exception to the general approach used to resolve proximate cause questions. I trust that you recall that, when analyzing a proximate cause question, the scope of a defendant's liability is measured by foreseeability; there is no liability for damages *of a type* that were unforeseeable given the breach. What the eggshell skull doctrine reveals is that there will be liability for damages that were unforeseeable *in degree.* Some emotional agitation is a foreseeable risk of careless driving, since by driving carelessly you could hit another car, and those in that other car would almost certainly be upset when their car is hit. Since the type of damage is foreseeable, defendant must pay for it even in cases where it turns out to be unforeseeably severe—psychosis instead of pissed-off-ness.

Although I have opted to mention the eggshell rule in a chapter labeled "Negligence: Damages," you should also be aware that it applies in all tort claims. If you have a pet wolverine and it scratches a guest in your home who just happens to have hemophilia and the guest bleeds to death, you will be liable for the death. The substantive claim would be predicated on strict liability for keeping a wild animal, but the eggshell rule applies. If you slap someone on the cheek and they go blind because of some peculiarity of the anatomy of their eyeballs, you will be liable for the blindness. The substantive claim would be an intentional tort (battery) but again the eggshell rule applies.

3. Allocation of Damages Between Multiple Defendants

Under the traditional common law approach, when a plaintiff established the liability of multiple defendants in the same case, those defendants were jointly liable to the plaintiff. What this meant was that plaintiff could collect the entire amount of the verdict against any one of the defendants. Plaintiff could choose the richest one, or the one with a local bank account, or even the one with the ugliest face. It was entirely the plaintiff's call.

Once the unlucky defendant paid the plaintiff, he had a right to seek some reimbursement from the other defendants in the case. This is called "contribution." Under the traditional approach, each co-defendant would be liable for an equal fractional share. This meant that if plaintiff recovered a judgement for $60,000 against Tom, Dick and Harry, and plaintiff opted to collect all the money from Tom, Tom could get $20,000 each from Dick and Harry. Of course, if either Dick or Harry was insolvent Tom would be out of luck, and would wind up getting stuck paying their share as well as his own. In other words, under the traditional rule, the risk of the insolvency of any one defendant was placed on the shoulders of the other defendants.

As the repeated use of the word "traditional" in the last two paragraphs likely suggested, a majority of states have changed this rule by statute. Under those statutes, the jury is instructed to assign each defendant a percentage of the total liability, and the defendants are each liable to the plaintiff only for that percentage of the total damages. Applying this rule in a three-defendant case, the jury might render a verdict that Tom was 10% at fault, Dick 30%, and Harry 60%. If the total damages were again $60,000, plaintiff could recover $6,000 from Tom, $18,000 from Dick, and $36,000 from Harry. Note that in this system, the risk of the insolvency of any one defendant is placed on the shoulders of the plaintiff. If Harry has no money, plaintiff will simply have to do without the $36,000 that Harry was obligated to pay; plaintiff cannot get this money from Tom or Dick.

In many states, the defendant or defendants can also argue that some percentage of fault should be assigned to parties who are not before the court. For instance, assume that a motel is sued for negligence. Plaintiff alleges that they did not adequately maintain a sliding glass door leading from her room to a patio, and that, as a result of this unreasonable conduct, an intruder was able to gain entry and assault the plaintiff. Assume the intruder was never caught. In this suit, the jury might determine that 80% of the fault should be assigned to the absent intruder while only 20% should be assigned to the motel. The result is that the plaintiff will not recover 80% of the damages. The legislature has determined that, as between the somewhat faulty motel-owner and the purely innocent motel-guest, it is better that the guest go undercompensated than that the motel owner should pay more than his "fair share." You may be able to guess my sentiments about this rule by the use of the quotation marks.

Note that in these modern systems of percentage allocation of fault there is no need for contribution claims between the defendants. Since no defendant has "overpaid" there is no need for adjustment between the defendants.

There are two situations, however, where a defendant who has paid the plaintiff can recover *all of the money* from a co-defendant. This is known as *indemnification*. The first of these involves cases where one defendant is vicariously liable and the other is liable as a direct or active tortfeasor. In such a case, if the vicariously liable party has paid some or all of the damages to the plaintiff, he can usually recover that full amount from the other defendant. Assume that Drambuie is a delivery person for Dhalia's Flower Shop and, en route to a wedding to deliver some flowers, he runs a red light and injures a pedestrian. The pedestrian sues both Drambuie—for his negligent act—and Dhalia as his boss on a theory of *respondeat superior*. After winning the case, plaintiff collects some or all of the money from Dhalia. Dhalia can get the money back from Drambuie.

The second situation where courts typically permit indemnification is in a strict products liability claim where one of the defendants is a non-manufacturer—typically a retailer. Say that Petrarch purchased a Cuisinart food processor from Macy's and that the first time he used it, the lid popped off and the S-shaped chopping blade lodged in his forehead. Petrarch would have a valid strict liability claim against both Cuisinart and Macy's. If he recovered some or all of his damages from Macy's, however, they could seek indemnification from Cuisinart and get all the money back. Effectively, this has the result of pushing the liability "upstream" onto the shoulders of the party which manufactured the product.

4. The Collateral Source Rule

Many individuals have medical insurance. Some also have disability insurance, which will pay a portion of the salary that is lost when an injury makes it impossible to work. Some even have rich relatives who will support them and pay their doctors if they get hurt. None of this operates to reduce the defendant's liability. Under what has come to be called the *collateral source rule* payments from these collateral sources are ignored in court. If plaintiff's damages total $75,000, but he received $30,000 in insurance payments in connection with the injury, the defendant still pays the full $75,000.

This may sound like quite a bonanza for plaintiffs, but in many cases the insurance company has a right to recover back from the plaintiff any money that it paid the plaintiff and that the plaintiff subsequently recovered in the lawsuit. Perhaps more relevant, however, is the fact that many jurisdictions have repealed the collateral source rule as part of the so-called "tort reform" movement that has periodically occupied state legislatures over the past decade or two. The result is that in these jurisdictions, the plaintiff's recovery *will* be reduced by any outside payments plaintiff has received. If the old rule was a potential bonanza for the plaintiff, the new one is something of a bonanza for defendants, who now pay less than the full damage they caused because of the lucky fact that they injured a person who happened to have insurance.

5. The Economic Loss Rule

It is sometimes said that one cannot recover in negligence for "pure" economic loss. Put as a positive statement, this means that there must be a physical injury to the plaintiff, or to an item of plaintiff's property, for there to be a valid negligence claim. For instance, assume a construction company is engaged in building a new skyscraper on an urban parcel of land and that, because of its negligence, one of its cranes drops a load of steel girders onto the street. No one is injured, but due to damage to the pavement, the street is closed to both vehicles and pedestrians for several days while the mess is cleaned up and the street is repaved. As a result, several businesses on the street lose revenue because patrons cannot get to their establishments. If those business owners were to sue the construction company, they would have no valid claim.[1]

Many academic writers and some courts have questioned whether a general and sweeping rule precluding recovery of "pure" economic loss actually exists. A large number of the cases denying recovery for pure economic loss can be explained just as easily by other doctrines. For instance, in some of the cases the defendant did not owe a duty of care to the person complaining of economic loss. In others, the economic loss was unforeseeable, meaning that the defendant's breach of duty was not, in the jargon, a "proximate cause" of the loss.

---

1 The hypothetical is based on *532 Madison Ave. Gourmet Foods, Inc. v. Finlandia Ctr., Inc.*, 96 N.Y.2d 280, 750 N.E.2d 1097 (2001).

When a defendant has a specific duty to take reasonable care to avoid inflicting economic losses, you will not be surprised to learn that plaintiffs are allowed to recover for those losses if that defendant is negligent, notwithstanding the "economic loss" rule. Assume a business hires an accounting firm to determine if a manager is engaged in embezzlement and that the accounting firm fails to conduct the audit in accordance with the professional standard of care. As a result, the manager is able to steal several thousand additional dollars. This is a "pure economic loss" but it is squarely within the scope of the duty of the accounting firm, and the business is clearly entitled to recover for the malpractice. Results in cases of this sort are sometimes justified by noting that there is a "special relationship" between the plaintiff and the defendant that trumps the pure-economic loss rule, but that may just be another way of saying that there is a duty of care in the specific situation that includes an obligation to avoid inflicting economic harm.

CHAPTER VIII

Defenses to Negligence Claims

1. Historical Evolution of Negligence Defenses

For the first two-thirds of the 20th century, there were two principal defenses a defendant could raise against a claim of negligence—contributory negligence and assumption of the risk. We can call these, collectively, the "traditional defenses." By the 1970's, however, states began abandoning the traditional defenses in favor of a doctrine known as comparative negligence.

At the present time, only a small number of jurisdictions retain the traditional defenses. In the case of contributory negligence, the number is down to five—mostly a cluster of states in the mid-Atlantic region. A slightly larger number continue to use the traditional assumption of risk doctrine, but as we shall see, in that connection there is some terminology that needs to be sorted through.

Although the traditional defenses are thus obsolete, the student of tort law may wish to know something about them out of intellectual curiosity, because he or she may plan to practice in one of the holdout states, or perhaps because he or she expects to see them on a final examination. We will therefore explore each of them in turn in the following sections of this chapter, and then turn our attention to the modern defense of comparative negligence to conclude the discussion.

2. The Mostly Obsolete Defense of Contributory Negligence

Contributory negligence is defined as the failure to use proper care for one's own safety. Each of us is obligated to use reasonable care for our own safety. We are all also supposed to obey statutes that have been enacted for our own safety. When we walk on the public streets, we are thus expected to watch where we are going, not jaywalk, not cross at a red light, and not yammer away on our cell phones oblivious of where we are or who is in our path. When we drive we are supposed to stop at red lights, pay attention, and avoid texting love notes to our main squeeze, not only to avoid injuring others, but for our own protection as well.

In a negligence suit a defendant may offer evidence of the plaintiff's contributory negligence (or contributory fault, as it is sometimes called). Under the traditional approach, if the jury believes this evidence, the plaintiff would recover nothing. Zero. In legal jargon, contributory negligence is an absolute bar to any recovery. While this rule had some slight advantages in ease of administration it was kind of . . . unfair. As a result, courts attempted to soften the impact of the doctrine with certain add-on rules. There are two that are worthy of note.

First, when the defendant had acted not just negligently, but *recklessly*, many courts would ignore the plaintiff's contributory negligence and permit the plaintiff to recover full damages. Thus, if an inattentive defendant-driver hit a jay-walking pedestrian-plaintiff, plaintiff would be barred and recover zero. But if a drunk driver doing 90 miles an hour in a residential neighborhood hit that same jay-walking pedestrian, plaintiff would recover fully.

The second exception to the usual absolute bar of contributory negligence was the *last clear chance* doctrine. This rule allowed a plaintiff to recover if, after his act of contributory negligence, the defendant still had an opportunity to avoid harm, but failed to take that opportunity. It was essentially a chronological concept—plaintiff's own negligent act is followed by an unreasonable act by defendant. Often, the plaintiff's act of carelessness in the last clear chance cases left him in a helpless position from which he could not escape, at which point the defendant could have prevented harm by the exercise of proper care.

Many of the last clear chance cases involve railroads or their urban cousins, subways. In a typical example, a drunk wanders onto railroad tracks and falls asleep there. A train comes barreling down those same tracks a few minutes later. If the engineer had been paying attention he would have seen the drunk dozing on the tracks and would have been able to apply emergency brakes in time to avoid an accident. Of course, it being a torts example, the engineer is not paying attention. He is reading a comic book, or gazing out a side window admiring the cows in an adjacent field. The result is that the sleeping drunk is killed. In the ensuing lawsuit, although the railroad could establish that the victim had been contributorily negligent, that contributory negligence would have been excused under the last clear chance rule.

3. The Mostly Obsolete Defense of Implied Assumption of the Risk

A plaintiff can waive his right to sue for negligence. When this is done after an injury, it is usually part of a settlement of the dispute. The defendant will give the plaintiff money, and the plaintiff then waives the right to go to court by executing a document called a "release."

The right to sue can also be waived *before* any negligent acts have taken place. Waivers of this sort are sometimes also called "express" assumption of the risk provisions. Such agreements are common in connection with various recreational activities, such as skiing or sky-diving. In some cases a court will refuse to enforce an express waiver if it would be contrary to public policy to do so. For instance, if an individual arrives at a hospital emergency room bleeding from a gunshot wound and the hospital refuses to admit him unless he signs a document waiving his right to sue the hospital for negligence, no court would enforce the document if the hospital carelessly transfused tainted blood or carelessly dropped the patient off of a stretcher.

Every state continues to treat an *express* assumption of the risk (or waiver) as a defense to a negligence claim, subject to the caveat about public policy just mentioned. However, a minority of states also recognize a traditional doctrine called *implied* assumption of the risk. Under this doctrine, *conduct* of the plaintiff that indicates a willingness to "take a chance" will operate to entirely bar any claim for negligence.

Under this increasingly obsolete defense, plaintiff's conduct was considered to signal an assumption of the risk where plaintiff knew that he was interacting with a negligent party, appreciated the associated risks of doing so, and chose to go ahead voluntarily. Some courts and text writers use the formula "knowing and voluntary" assumption of the risk to capture these key points. Traditional implied assumption of the risk was an absolute bar to recovery. Here is one of the several examples provided by the Restatement of Torts:

> *A, a storekeeper, fails to put a guard around an open trap door in the floor of his poorly lighted shop, or to give any warning of it. B, entering the shop, sees the opening, and realizes that because of the slippery condition of the floor around it he may fall through it. B nevertheless proceeds to stand near the edge of the opening in order to look at goods on shelves behind it. He slips, falls through, and is hurt. B may be found to have assumed the risk.*

Let us ignore for a moment the question of what kind of odd store contains a trap door in the middle of the floor. Note that in this example, the storekeeper is not acting in a reasonably prudent fashion—the store is poorly lighted, and there is no warning of the open trap door. A customer who inadvertently fell through the trap door without noticing it in advance would surely have a good cause of action for negligence. This particular customer, however, has full knowledge of the risk—he sees the opening, knows the floor is slippery, and "realizes" that he may fall through. He then voluntarily chooses to encounter the risk because of his intense desire to inspect the goods on the shelving behind the gaping hole in the floor. This conduct communicates the implied message that he waives any claim for negligence should he get hurt.

Implied assumption of the risk often drives law students crazy. That is because, in a very large number of cases, it looks just like contributory negligence. In the Restatement example, one might say that it is not reasonably prudent to stand on a slippery floor at the very edge of an open trap door for the relatively unimportant purpose of inspecting some goods on a shelf.

If there is a distinction it is subtle. The assumption of the risk situation implies some consent or waiver, while contributory negligence involves a type of unknowing carelessness by plaintiff that does not implicate consent. Think back to the jaywalking plaintiff—our poster child of contributory negligence. Such a plaintiff clearly is not being adequately careful for his own safety. However, this plaintiff cannot be said to consent to getting hit by a car. He is not OK with that. In the assumption of the risk cases the plaintiff is daring, audacious, or cocky, while in the contributory negligence cases he is stupidly oblivious or unaware.

The good news is that with the advent of comparative negligence—to which we will turn momentarily—none of this matters much any more. The vast majority of states have abolished both traditional contributory negligence, and traditional implied assumption of the risk, so the effort to pull them apart is no longer necessary. There is, however, one lingering use of the "assumption of the risk" terminology that continues to haunt the cases. It is sufficiently common, and sufficiently cryptic, to require its own subsection.

4. Primary Assumption of the Risk

As we saw much earlier, the general duty of "reasonable care under the circumstances" does not apply in every situation. In addition to the special duty rules we considered in Chapter 3, the ordinary duty of care does not apply in the context of athletic or sporting competitions.

Take baseball. Let us consider what would follow if the law set the duty of a baseball player as "reasonable prudence under the circumstances." A reasonable person knows that striking the ball with full force could result in a line drive directly at the pitcher, causing an injury. The benefit or utility of striking the ball with full force is pretty minimal—it's just a silly game after all. The burden of giving the ball just a gentle tap is virtually zero. Under a reasonable prudence approach, therefore, baseball players should not play hard. That, however, would take all the fun out of the game. It is a competition and if players are not exerting their maximum effort it would destroy the whole point.

Consequently, most courts would say that the only duty owed by a participant in a baseball game to others on the field is a duty to refrain from reckless conduct. Thus, if the pitcher is hit by a line drive and sues the batter, the batter cannot be held liable merely because he swung for the fences. This accords (hopefully) with your common sense notions. In such a lawsuit most people would say that the batter "did nothing wrong," "acted like he was supposed to," or if they were inclined to legal language, "was not negligent."

Regrettably, the courts do not use this straightforward language. Instead, they say that the pitcher who got hit by the ball cannot recover because he "assumed the risk." More specifically, they call this "primary" assumption of the risk. (The kind of assumption of risk considered in the previous section is, thus, sometimes more fully labelled "secondary" assumption of the risk.) What this means is that the pitcher agreed to participate in an activity where others owed him a duty lower than the ordinary standard of reasonable care under the circumstances. Since others players are not obligated to use reasonable care, there is naturally a heightened risk of injury. It is that risk that the pitcher assumes.

The idea of primary assumption of risk is often extended to spectators at athletic contests. Thus, fans at hockey games who get hit by a puck or spectators at a golf match who get hit by a golf ball are typically denied recovery. The players who hit the puck or golf ball have not done anything other than play the game as it should be played in order to make it exciting and competitive. The owner of the hockey rink is not expected to extend barriers entirely over the ice in some sort of dome-like structure because it would interfere with fans' ability to see and hear the game. The only duty owed is to play the game "normally" and avoid reckless acts, and thus there is no breach of duty that the injured spectator can point to as a basis for recovery.

If you have followed me thus far, you will realize that primary assumption of the risk is not really an affirmative defense at all. Rather, it is a concise way of saying "reduced duty, hence no breach." It is unfortunate that courts use language that is so evocative of the implied (or secondary) assumption of the risk defense considered in the previous section, but that's just the way it is with courts sometimes.

5. Comparative Negligence

As we have seen, the two "traditional" affirmative defenses—contributory negligence and implied assumption of the risk—have been abolished in most jurisdictions. They have been replaced by the more modern doctrine known as comparative negligence (sometimes also called comparative fault).

Under comparative fault, when a defendant proves that the plaintiff has failed to take adequate precautions for his own safety, the jury will be instructed to weigh the fault of the plaintiff against the fault of the defendant; in other words, to compare their respective degrees of fault (hence the name). The jury will assign each of the parties a percentage reflecting its assessment of fault. There are no firm guidelines that govern this percentage-assigning process. The jury is largely on its own. To make it concrete, assume that we have a drunk driver who hit a jaywalker and that the jury assigns 80% of the fault to the driver and 20% to the jaywalker.

The consequence is that the plaintiff's recovery will be reduced by his own percentage of fault. If the jaywalker had proved a total of $150,000 in damages, he would forfeit 20% of that amount, and only be entitled to recover $120,000. In some states, if the plaintiff is found to be more than 50% at fault, he will recover nothing. This system is called modified or partial comparative negligence. In states where it is in effect there is sometimes a dispute whether the jury should be informed about the rule. Obviously, a jury that is aware that a 60% negligent plaintiff will go home with no recovery at all may be strongly inclined to "adjust" the percentages to avoid that result. Where the jurisdiction goes strictly by the percentages and always allows the plaintiff to obtain at least some recovery, the system is called "pure" comparative negligence.

Under either form of comparative negligence, all the subsidiary rules that cluttered the traditional landscape are swept away. There is no longer any need for a last clear chance doctrine. There is no longer a special rule for cases where the defendant is reckless while the plaintiff is merely negligent. Rather, everything now goes "in the hopper" to be considered by the jury in its allocation of fault percentages. The evidence remains relevant but the rules drop away.

Even under comparative negligence, however, there are some situations where we may have an "all or nothing" outcome instead of a "split the baby based on the percentages" approach. One such scenario is when the duty of the defendant is to protect the plaintiff from his own careless behavior. In such a case it would be inappropriate to reduce the plaintiff's recovery because of his carelessness. In these cases plaintiff recovers 100% of his damages.

For instance, let us say that Purvis has been hospitalized for an ailment, one symptom of which is forgetfulness. Assume that he is prescribed medication which he is instructed to take on his own three times a day. As you would predict, because of his absent-mindedness, he forgets several doses and suffers complications. He sues the hospital claiming that they were negligent in having him take the medication on his own—he says they should have sent a nurse to his room to administer the medication. The hospital lawyer argues in response that Purvis was comparatively negligent for failing to take the medication. This is a pretty lame argument. The whole theory of Purvis's case is that he was dependent on the hospital to see to it that he got the medication *because he would not likely remember to take it on his own.* It would be illogical and almost cruel to call his failure comparative negligence in a case like this.

A rather different scenario can arise where the plaintiff's negligent conduct causes a type of harm entirely different than the one foreseeably associated with defendant's breach. In the unhappy language that I tried desperately to avoid in the Proximate Cause chapter, plaintiff's carelessness in these cases is what courts call a "superceding cause." In these cases, plaintiff does not recover a percentage of his damages; rather he will recover nothing at all.

An example of this kind of situation might be where Dagwood invites Pierre to stay at his home while he is out of town.

There is a pool in the backyard, and there are no depth markings on the side of the pool. Pierre, however, has used the pool every day of his stay and knows which end of the pool is the shallow end. On the last day of his stay, he dives head first into the shallow end of the pool with predictable consequences. He then sues Dagwood claiming the failure to have the depth markings as a breach. However, the risk associated with that breach is that someone *unfamiliar* with the pool might dive into the shallow end. That someone who knew the depth would do so is unforeseeable. Thus, Pierre would likely recover nothing in this case—his injuries are outside the scope of Dagwood's responsibility and it would be unfair to hold Dagwood liable for any damages. The comparative negligence doctrine would not apply and Pierre would not be eligible for a partial recovery.

CHAPTER IX

Strict Liability For Defective Products

1. Introductory Observations

Modern society brings us into constant contact with manufactured products. At home, most of us use a wide range of kitchen appliances, power tools, home electronics, and grooming devices. We all eat processed food products and virtually all of us eventually take over-the-counter or prescription drugs. The vast majority of us drive a car, and many of us use other vehicles for recreation such as snowmobiles, ATVs, or jet skis. We use sporting equipment like golf clubs, tennis racquets, exercise equipment, or even football helmets. At work, we may drive a fork-lift truck, use a meat slicer, or operate a drill press, or wear specialized gear such as goggles or safety gloves. Most of these objects have the potential to injure us if there is something wrong with them.

When a seller has manufactured or assembled such a product carelessly, that seller can be sued for negligence under the rules, limitations and principles we have examined in earlier chapters. Even if the injured party is not exactly sure what negligent act—what "breach"—took place, the doctrine of *res ipsa loquitur* may allow him to go forward. In addition, the victim may be able to make a breach of warranty claim concerning the product under the provisions of the Uniform Commercial Code, which you have likely encountered in a course on Contracts.

In addition, an injured party can also assert a strict liability claim, which we will examine in detail momentarily. Be aware that when texts on the law of torts speak of "products liability" without the use of qualifications or additional adjectives, they are likely referring to the full range of potential theories on which product sellers might be held legally accountable. When texts speak of "*strict* products liability," however, they are usually confining the conversation to a claim predicated on, you guessed it, strict liability alone. This chapter is about strict products liability.

The historical evolution of the strict liability claim is largely a story of slow judicial abandonment of various prerequisites that made other causes of action impractical for many plaintiffs. We can think of the modern strict liability claim as requiring a plaintiff to prove four elements: (1) Defendant was a merchant; (2) the product was defective; (3) the product has not been altered since leaving defendant's control; and (4) the plaintiff was making a foreseeable use of the product. Each of these elements requires some elaboration to give the full flavor of the cause of action, so let us consider them in separate sub-sections.

2. Defendant Must Be a Merchant

Only a merchant—sometimes also called a commercial distributor—can be held strictly liable for injuries caused by a defective product. A merchant is someone who normally deals in goods of the type that injured the plaintiff. A party need not actually *sell* goods to be considered a merchant. Commercial lessors, like rental car companies, or companies that rent furniture are also merchants, and can be held strictly liable.

Service providers sometimes make tangible goods available as an incidental part of rendering their services. Nonetheless, they do not deal in those goods, and are not considered merchants of them. Thus, if you go to your accountant's office to discuss your annual tax return and get injured when you sit down on a chair there, you will not be able to succeed on a strict liability claim against him. He is not in the business of dealing in chairs. "Casual" sellers are also not considered merchants and thus are not vulnerable to strict liability claims. Typical examples of casual sellers would be persons selling used goods online, or at a garage sale, or a business selling off surplus equipment as part of a down-sizing.

All parties in a chain of distribution are considered to be merchants. That means that a strict liability claim can be asserted not just against the retailer from whom a consumer purchased a product, but against the wholesaler and the manufacturer as well. A strict liability claim can even be asserted against the supplier of a component part that proved defective. Thus, the plaintiff is not limited to suing only the party with whom he dealt directly. In the formal language of the law, there is no requirement of "privity of contract."

3. The Product Must Be Defective

It is often said that a major difference between negligence and strict products liability is that the former focuses on the conduct of the defendant while the latter focuses on the condition of the product. That is why the second element of a strict liability claim requires the plaintiff to show that the product had some kind of defect which made it unreasonably dangerous to the user.

There are three different kinds of defects recognized by the case law. The first is known as a *manufacturing defect*—sometimes also called a production flaw. A product has a manufacturing defect when it differs or departs from its intended design in a way that makes it more dangerous than a consumer would expect. The fact that the manufacturer exercised reasonable care in producing and inspecting the product is irrelevant. A product with a manufacturing flaw is the "bad one that slipped through." The one-in-a-million car whose brakes or steering fail when you get 10 miles from the dealership; or the one-in-a-million can of tuna fish with a sharp shard of metal in the can would be classic examples.

The second kind of defect is known as a *design defect*. Originally, courts attempted to define design defects in terms of consumer expectations—on this view a product was considered defectively designed if it was more dangerous than a consumer, with ordinary knowledge common to the community, would expect. This test proved troublesome for several reasons. For some products, consumers did not have enough experience to have any expectations one way or the other about safety. For others, especially those used in industrial settings, users may have become so familiar with the product's dangers that the product was not *more* dangerous than they expected, even though it was very dangerous and could easily have been made safer.

Given these difficulties, many courts, and the current Restatement of Products Liability, use a "risk-benefit" or "risk-utility" test to define a design defect. Under this test, the product is defective in design if a reasonable seller with knowledge of its dangers would not have placed it on the market, which is another way of saying that its risks outweigh its utility or benefits to users.

Plaintiffs can prove defective design by showing that there was an alternative way the product could have been built which meets three conditions. First, the alternative would have been safer than the version actually marketed. Second, the alternative would have cost consumers approximately the same amount of money as the version actually marketed. Finally, the alternative is practical, meaning that it does not make the product difficult to use, or undermine its primary purpose. This approach is endorsed by the Restatement (Third) of Products Liability, but some courts and academic writers have criticized it for imposing an unduly high burden on plaintiffs.

One of the best known and most frequently cited examples of a defectively designed product is the Ford Pinto automobile that was sold in the early 1970's. That car had a gas tank placed under the rear-most portion of the vehicle—essentially under the rear bumper. The result was that the car had the unfortunate tendency to explode when struck from behind in an accident. This is more dangerous than most consumers expect from their car. Moreover, evidence suggested that the car could have been redesigned with the gas tanker further forward. This would have been safer because the explosion risk would have been greatly reduced. Moreover, it would not have cost a great deal of money to move the gas tank and doing so would not have made the car difficult to build or operate or have had any other significant negative consequences. It is therefore a kind of car that a reasonable seller would not put on the market.

Let me make two closing observations about design defects. First, if the risk-utility test sounds a lot like negligence, that is because it is, essentially, negligence. Although courts will sometimes say that a merchant is strictly liable for selling a product that is defective in design, the only way to prove that the product was defective in design is to show that the seller was unreasonable in selling it. If this strikes you as either confusing or disingenuous, I am right there with you. But as the popular saying of the moment goes, it is what it is.

The other observation about design defects is that where a design defect exists, *every unit* of a production run is defective and thus *every unit* is a lawsuit waiting to happen. This is in stark contrast to manufacturing defect cases where only a single unit out of thousands that may have been sold, has the dangerous, attributes that might lead to injury or litigation. This is not a new bit of law, but rather just a by-product of the definitions used for the two categories. It does mean, however, that the stakes for sellers are much higher in the design defect context.

The final kind of defect recognized by the cases is an information defect. If a product has risks that could not be eliminated by a practical design change, and if those risks would not be obvious to users, the product is defective unless it contains adequate warnings and instructions. To be "adequate" warnings and instructions must be sufficiently prominent to come to the attention of the user; must be in clear language; and may have to be bilingual or in pictures to be sure that users who do not read English can appreciate the dangers. So, if an over-the-counter medication can cause serious side effects if it is taken in combination with other drugs, and if there is no way to reformulate that medication to avoid the problem, the medication needs a warning. If it is sold without the warning, it would be defective.

Warnings do not automatically insulate sellers from liability. If a product's risk could be eliminated by an inexpensive and practical re-design, sellers cannot escape liability by slapping a warning on the product. A bumper sticker on the Pinto that said "Will Explode in the Event of Rear End Collision" might give consumers better information, but we really would prefer that the manufacturer spend twenty bucks per car and relocate the gas tank to avoid the potential for explosions.

4. The Product Must Not Have Been Altered

For a seller to be held strictly liable, the defective product must reach the consumer without a substantial change in the condition in which it was sold. The defect must, therefore, have existed at the time the product left the defendant's hands.

Assume that Priscilla purchases a Sunbeam brand clothes iron from her local Wal-Mart store. Following the instructions, she fills it with water, plugs it in, turns it on and gets ready to iron her favorite blouse, whereupon the iron shoots a stream of boiling hot water directly into her eye, causing her permanent loss of vision. She files a strict liability claim against Sunbeam, the manufacturer, alleging a manufacturing defect. Priscilla would have to prove that the problem that caused the jet of scalding water to shoot from the iron existed when the iron left Sunbeam's factory. That, of course, is not inevitable. For instance, an employee of the trucking company that shipped the iron to Wal-Mart could have dropped that particular iron, which might have caused the problem. Or employees of Wal-Mart could have left that particular iron out on the loading dock on a rainy day and the humidity could have caused a short circuit.

Indeed, the more you think about this requirement, the harder Priscilla's task will seem. She would have to find everyone who handled the product after it left Sunbeam and get them to testify that they didn't do anything—either deliberately or accidentally—to alter its condition. That could be very burdensome, maybe even impossible.

Recognizing the difficulty, courts have decided that the fact of non-alteration can be presumed, in any case where the product moved in ordinary channels of distribution. "Ordinary channels" simply means that the product was bought from a conventional retailer who got it either directly from the manufacturer, or through a wholesaler. The presumption means that the burden is on Sunbeam to offer affirmative evidence of some kind of alteration, if it exists, and if they do not do so, the element is deemed satisfied.

Note that the presumption does not apply if the product is purchased second-hand, for instance at a garage sale. That would not be "ordinary channels of distribution." In such a case, Priscilla would indeed bear the burden of showing non-alteration.

5. The User Was Making a Foreseeable Use of the Product

In order to recover in a strict products liability suit, the user must have been using the product in a foreseeable fashion at the time of injury. This does not necessarily mean that the user was using the product properly or appropriately. Many misuses of products are entirely foreseeable. It is arguably a misuse of a car to drive at 90 miles an hour, but it is totally foreseeable that at least some users of a car will do exactly that. If, when the car gets to that speed, it begins to vibrate so violently that the driver loses control, the car manufacturer cannot escape liability by arguing that the driver was "misusing" the vehicle.

Under this same analysis, getting into an accident with your car would also be a "misuse," but since accidents happen all the time, they are nonetheless foreseeable. That means that cars must be designed to take accidents into account. They must have a range of cost-justified and practical safety features that will protect occupants in the event of a crash. This is sometimes called the "crashworthiness" doctrine.

Of course, some people do manage to use products in entirely unforeseeable ways. When they do, they will not be able to recover. The individual who uses a steam iron to try to sear pimples off of his face is making what, I think we can all agree, is an unforeseeable use. When he appears in court, face adorned with severe burns, claiming that the iron was defective because it should have had an automatic shut-off feature, his case will be dead on arrival.

6. Defenses to Strict Products Liability Claims

With the widespread adoption of comparative negligence around the country, many jurisdictions have moved to a similar doctrine in the area of strict products liability. In the strict liability context this doctrine is usually called "comparative responsibility," because the defendant is not, technically speaking, negligent. Despite the different name, however, its operation is identical to what we saw previously in Chapter 8. Any plaintiff fault—including an unreasonable failure to discover the product defect, or the use of the product after the defect has been discovered—will result in an assignment of some percentage of responsibility to the plaintiff for the injury. The plaintiff's recovery is then reduced by that percentage.

Some jurisdictions continue to follow an older or more traditional approach to defenses. Under this system a plaintiff's failure to discover the defect, even if unreasonable (we could call this "oblivious contributory negligence") is disregarded and plaintiff recovers 100% of his damages. On the other hand, plaintiff's decision to use the product once the defect is known (we could call this "assumption of the risk") is treated as an absolute bar to recovery, and the plaintiff recovers nothing. As noted, the number of states that make this kind of distinction is on the wane.

CHAPTER X

Other Strict Liability Claims

1. Abnormally Dangerous Activities

In an old English case called *Rylands v. Fletcher,* Mr. Fletcher bought some land in an area that was devoted to coal mining. Indeed, the land still had a large number of abandoned vertical mine shafts that connected to several mines below the surface, and that had been filled up with dirt and rubbish, though apparently neither Fletcher nor anyone else know about these. Fletcher wanted to build a mill for grinding wheat or other grains into flour. At that time, the millstones that did this grinding were powered by water which cascaded down onto paddle wheels. The water, in turn, was kept readily at hand in a "millpond." If you can't see what's coming next in this story, you haven't read enough torts cases.

Fletcher built a mill pond, but the weight of the water was too much for the ground, because of all those old mine shafts.

The result was that the ground collapsed and a coal mine owned by Mr. Rylands was flooded. Rylands was not pleased. Outfitting his miners with scuba gear was not in his plans. So he sued. The case wound up in the House of Lords, which was then the highest tribunal in the land. Although there was no finding of any negligence by Fletcher, their Lordships found him liable nonetheless. The theory was that he was engaged in a "non-natural" use of his property, which meant that he acted "at his peril" if the result was harm to his neighbors.

That case—with some twists and turns—is the origin of the current rule imposing strict liability on those who engage in *abnormally dangerous* activities. Under the modern definition, an activity is considered abnormally dangerous if it meets two tests. First, it must create a foreseeable risk of serious harm even when reasonable care is exercised. In other words, normal or ordinary care will not eliminate the chance of a fairly significant harm. This is just a verbose way of saying that the activity is abnormally dangerous! Second, the activity must be one which is uncommon in the place where it is being conducted. In other words it is out of context, much as Fletcher's millpond was out of place in the middle of a region devoted to coal mining. In more casual language, therefore, an activity is abnormally dangerous if it is highly risky and if no one else is doing it in this particular location.

Common examples of abnormally dangerous activities include the use of explosives, working with large quantities of highly toxic substances such as dangerous chemicals or biological agents, and in some cases, the use of radioactive or nuclear materials (though in these cases some state claims can be preempted by federal statutes dealing with the control of nuclear material).

When an activity qualifies as abnormally dangerous, the person carrying on the activity will be liable to anyone injured by that activity, regardless of his safety precautions. That, of course, is the meaning of strict liability. Thus, even if one conducts blasting operations with the utmost care, those who are injured will have a claim. In most jurisdictions, however, a plaintiff's recovery will be reduced by his own comparative fault. If a plaintiff ignores warning signs about blasting operations and chooses to approach very near the site of the blasting to get a better look at the excitement, the plaintiff is, to be a bit blunt, something of an idiot, and it is likely that the jury will assign him a considerable percentage of the blame in connection with his own injuries.

2. Keeping Animals

A person who keeps a "wild" animal will be strictly liable for any harm done by the creature. According to the Restatement, a wild animal is any animal "not by custom devoted to the service of mankind at the time and in the place in which it is kept." Felines seem to feature heavily in the cases. There has been litigation involving bobcats, cougars and even tigers. Of course, other wild animals have made cameo appearances. One Massachusetts case from the 1960's held an animal fair strictly liable for injuries caused by an escaped zebra, which apparently was running loose on the streets of the city of Springfield. They are probably still talking about that to this very day.

Strict liability is also imposed in some states for harm done by trespassing livestock. In these states if your cattle or sheep leave your property, go on your neighbors land, and eat his crops, you will be liable, even if you took all reasonable precautions to prevent such a thing from happening. Even in these jurisdictions, however, there is no liability for harm done by cattle that stray off of a road onto adjoining property—in that situation the owner will only be liable for negligence. In other states, however, property owners have the obligation of "fencing out" livestock, and if they have failed to erect fences to protect their own crop land they will not be able to recover.

Outside of the trespassing livestock situation, one is otherwise not strictly liable for harm done by domesticated animals such as the typical house pet or farm animal. Thus, if your dog bites a house guest you can only be held liable if the guest can prove some sort of negligence on your part. However, there is an exception to this rule. If you have prior knowledge that your domesticated animals have dangerous propensities, strict liability will be imposed. In the case of dogs, such knowledge is usually assumed if the dog previously has bitten someone, though it can be found based other facts as well. This is the origin of the quaint saying that "every dog gets one free bite." Of course, the dog actually gets as many free bites as he wants; the one bite limit applies to the owner.

Finally, we should note an "exception to the exception." Even if you have knowledge of the vicious propensities of a domesticated animal, you will not be strictly liable if it injures a trespasser on your own property. In other words, if you have—and know you have—a dog with vicious propensities, you will be strictly liable if it bites a social guest in your home, or a passerby on the street when you take the critter out for a walk, but not to an intruder who enters your home without permission.

CHAPTER XI

Dignitary, Economic and Other Torts

1. Defamation

An ancient Roman writer, Publilius Syrus, is reputed to have said "a good reputation is more valuable than money." While the existence of the Kardashians may cast doubt on his observation, the law of Torts honors this idea with the cause of action for defamation.

In order to make out a traditional defamation claim a plaintiff is obligated to prove three things: (1) the defendant made a "defamatory" statement that specifically identified the plaintiff; (2) the defendant published that statement; and (3) that there are either presumed or "special" damages, depending on the kind of case. Some states also require that the defendant made the statement in other than good faith—in other words, that there be proof of some kind of culpable state of mind or fault.

The key aspect of the first element is determining what kind of statements qualify as "defamatory." The rule is that a statement meets the test if it tends to adversely affect one's reputation. That means that the statement lowers the plaintiff in the esteem of the community and deters others from associating with him. Other courts get more flowery and say that a statement is defamatory when it exposes the plaintiff to hatred, ridicule, contempt, or disgrace. Under this test, mere insults of a conclusory nature are not actionable.

The typical defamatory statement is thus cast as an assertion of fact—something like "Petruccio killed a man in Texas last month," or "Professor Petrarch never went to college and forged his credentials to get his teaching job." In addition, a statement in the form of an opinion will also be considered defamatory if it would suggest to a listener that it is based on facts. On the other hand, a purely subjective statement of opinion is not considered defamatory. For instance a statement by a restaurant reviewer that "in my opinion the meatballs at Casa Pisa are the worst in town," would not qualify as defamatory. That statement clearly reflects nothing more than the judgment of the reviewer.

A statement need not be defamatory "on its face." The plaintiff is permitted to offer additional evidence to show that, in context, listeners would take away a defamatory meaning. For instance, assume that Donatello says that "whenever Porter visits Chicago he stays at the DelMonaco Hotel." This hardly seems defamatory. Who cares what hotel Porter prefers? However, if Porter claims that everyone knows that the DelMonaco is a brothel, and can prove that fact, he will be able to go forward in a defamation suit.

The first element of the defamation tort also requires that the statement specifically identify the plaintiff or, as some older cases say, be "of and concerning" the plaintiff. In the first instance, this means that only the person named in the statement will have a claim—others who may suffer collateral harm to their reputations are out of luck. Thus the statement that Dr. Parker is not competent may injure the reputation of the Chief of Surgery who hired him, but only Parker will be able bring suit.

Where the statement refers to the plaintiff by name the requirement of identity is plainly satisfied. It would also be satisfied by other references sufficient to pinpoint a specific individual. Thus if someone were to say that "the U.S. Attorney for the Western District of Kansas is on the payroll of the mob," that adequately identifies a specific individual even though no name is used, since the identity of the U.S. Attorney for the district in question is readily ascertainable.

If the statement refers to all members of a group, the size of the group in question will determine if the statement satisfies the first element. Where the group is small, the assumption is that all members of the group have suffered a reputational harm, and thus all could sue. An example might be the statement that "one of the waitresses at Mel's Diner is a prostitute," where there are only three waitresses who work at that establishment. However, when the group is large, a statement referencing it does not point with enough specificity at any one person, and thus no one will have a defamation claim. Thus, if the statement is that "one of the persons who passed the New York bar exam last summer cheated on the exam," none of the 11,000 individuals who took that test would have a valid cause of action.

Two final points of interest regarding the first element of defamation are worthy of note. First, the plaintiff need not be a "natural" person. A corporation can be defamed, though obviously some kinds of defamatory statements relevant to individuals would be incoherent if applied to corporations (for instance "Microsoft has committed adultery three time last month" does not make very much sense, other than suggesting some kind of weird relationship with Apple). Second, the plaintiff must have been alive at the time the defendant made the statement, which means that as a practical matter you can speak with impunity about a dead person.

The second element of defamation is the publication requirement. This requires plaintiff to prove that defendant disclosed the statement to at least one person other than the plaintiff himself. The logic here is that your reputation cannot be hurt if the only person to hear the negative statement is you, because your reputation is what *other people* think of you.

Note, however, that the requirement of publication is *de minimis*. It does not require that the defendant share the statement with a large number of persons and it certainly does not require publication in the sense of reproduction in a book, newspaper or magazine. If Dragan tells his friend John that "Pavel is a member of a terrorist organization" that will be enough for Pavel to establish publication in a suit against Dragan. Of course the more persons who hear the statement, the greater the likely reputational damage, and the more money plaintiff will recover. The point remains, however, that all the plaintiff must show to avoid a directed verdict is that the statement was shared with one person other than himself.

Indeed, publication need not even be intentional. It is enough if the defendant negligently disclosed the statement to another person. For instance, if Dave calls Pete to his office and accuses him of filing false expense reports, but has negligently left his intercom on so that his secretary hears the entire conversation, that will count as publication.

Those who "republish" a defamatory statement will be just as vulnerable to liability as the person who first published it. There is no defense available to the person who claims to just be repeating what he heard from someone else.

The last of the standard requirements for recovery is proof of damages. In many cases, however, damages are presumed, which effectively means that this element drops out of the case. The first category of cases where the law presumes damages are known as *libel* cases. A libel is a defamatory statement that is in writing or in some other permanent format such as on videotape. It is libel when Dirk sends a letter to his brother Kirk and says in the letter that his boss Patrick is embezzling from the company where he works. It is also libel when the New York Times publishes a statement on the front page that Senator Pullman is taking bribes. Although the plaintiff in a libel case is not *obligated* to put on evidence of damages, he remains free to do so, and as you might expect, the more damage you prove, the more money the jury is likely to award. Consequently, the plaintiff who relies on the rule of presumed damages may make it to the jury but find himself the unsatisfied recipient of a very paltry damage award.

The second situation where there is a presumption of damage involves the so-called *slander per se* cases. A slander is a spoken or oral defamatory statement. Slanders are considered to fall into the per se category if they relate to one of four itemized subjects. Specifically, a statement is slander per se if (1) it relates to the plaintiff's business or profession; (2) it declares that the plaintiff has committed a crime of moral turpitude; (3) it says that the plaintiff suffers from a loathsome disease; or (4) it imputes unchastity to a woman. If most of these categories seem to have a medieval feel to them, that is because these rules are several centuries old and come down to us almost unchanged from the pre-Colonial law of England.

If you have been following the story, this means that there is only one type of defamation case where a plaintiff must actually prove special damages to get to the jury—a slander case not falling into one of the four per se categories. In these cases, courts require proof of an economic or pecuniary harm. Examples would be that the plaintiff was fired because her employer heard the defamatory statement, or that patronage has fallen off at the plaintiff's restaurant because of what the defendant said about him. Harm of a purely social sort is not sufficient. Once pecuniary harm is proved, however, the plaintiff is then entitled to any emotional harm associated with that loss. This means that if the plaintiff was fired the jury can award damages both for the loss of wages and for the distress and humiliation associated with losing employment.

Some states also require proof of special damages in cases involving what is called libel *per quod*. This is a libel that is not defamatory "on its face" and which thus requires additional context to make out its reputation-harming effect. The example several paragraphs above involving a statement that Parker stays at the Hotel DelMonaco when he goes to Chicago would, if written down, be libel per quod.

2. Defenses to Defamation Claims

Consent is a defense to a claim of defamation, although the situations where this is likely to be relevant are rather rare. Imagine, however, that a supervisor writes a critical review of a subordinate and asks the subordinate to read it, to indicate if it contains any errors, and to sign it if correct. Assume that the subordinate signs the review with no changes and the review is then shared with others in the organization. In this case, any claim of defamation will be barred by the subordinate's consent.

More importantly, truth is also a defense to a claim of defamation. The defendant in a defamation case will escape liability if he can prove that the substance of the statement he made is accurate. Note that because it is an affirmative defense, the burden of proof on this issue will lie with the defendant.

There are also a number of privilege defenses that can be used to avoid liability in defamation cases. Some of these are considered "absolute" privileges. There are two that are worthy of particular note. The first is for communications between spouses. If Darrin says to his wife "my boss is stealing money from the company," he cannot be sued by the boss, because the only person to whom he published the statement is his spouse. The second absolute privilege applies to statements made by government officials in the course of their official duties. This privilege is particularly important in the judicial context where it covers statements made not merely by judges, but those of attorneys and witnesses as well. Because of this privilege a lawyer cannot be liable for defamation because of anything she says during her opening or closing statements at trial, or for any statements that appear in a pleading, brief or other document submitted to the court.

Another well-recognized privilege is the so-called "fair reporting" privilege. Members of the print and broadcast media are allowed to make accurate reports of public proceedings such as trials or legislative hearings, and have immunity for reprinting what was said at those proceedings, so long as their report is accurate.

In addition, the cases recognize a qualified privilege in any situation where there is a public interest in encouraging candor. For instance, when a business owner provides an evaluation of a former employee who is seeking a new job, when a bank provides an evaluation of the creditworthiness of a borrower, or when a citizen talks to the police, we do not want them to hold back negative information. So, to give them some confidence that they can speak without risk of getting sued, the law provides a privilege. This privilege, however, is subject to two conditions.

First, the defendant must have made the alleged defamatory statement "in good faith." This means that the defendant had a reasonable belief that the statement was true. (The statement will, of course, *not* be true—if it were true, truth would be a defense and we would not need to even think about the privilege concept). To put this same point the other way around, a defendant will lose a qualified privilege if he is deliberately spreading a lie, or making reckless or negligent statements about the plaintiff.

Second, the defendant must confine his comments to matters relevant to the purpose that justifies the privilege in the first place. The privilege is not a license to simply gossip at random about the plaintiff. If the banker, in response to a call about Parker's credit, also chooses to mention the fact that whenever Parker comes into the bank he is with a different women and that therefore he is probably committing adultery, the banker cannot rely on a privilege when Parker sues, since Parker's sexual escapades are not relevant to his creditworthiness.

3. The Public Concern Defamation Scenario

The threat of a defamation suit is a powerful weapon. It can intimidate many folks into keeping their mouths shut. However, this kind of intimidation is at odds with First Amendment values that seek to encourage robust debate about matters of public importance. Because of this, the U.S. Supreme Court has held that there must be limits on the defamation cause of action to avoid "chilling" free speech. These limits arise whenever the subject matter of a statement is a matter of *public concern.*

Neither the Supreme Court nor very many other courts have attempted a general definition of the term "public concern," choosing instead to decide whether a particular challenged statement falls within the concept on a case-by-case basis. One federal appellate court has said that statements about "the public acts and qualifications of public officials and candidates; the management of educational, charitable and religious institutions; public offerings of a literary, artistic and scientific nature; [and] public offerings of products for use and consumption" certainly meet the test.

In many cases involving alleged defamatory statements relating to a matter of public concern the defendant has been a media company—a newspaper, perhaps, or a television station. Of course, with the advent of the Internet, virtually everyone is now in a position to offer up their opinions, not just about the shortcomings of their neighbors and their co-workers, but also about politicians, civic leaders and consumer products. Thus, nowadays the defendant in a public concern defamation case could just as easily be a teenage blogger as the *New York Times*.

In cases involving matters of public concern, the plaintiff is obligated to prove two extra elements in order to establish defamation. The first of these is *falsity.* Let us assume that a newspaper publishes a story reporting that a member of the state legislature—let's call him Pendleton—has taken bribes in exchange for his votes. Pendleton has now sued the newspaper for defamation. Because the question of the honesty of a public official is definitely a matter of public concern Pendleton would be obligated to prove that he has not taken bribes. In effect, the statement in the newspaper would be presumed true and Pendleton would bear the burden of showing otherwise.

The second extra element that arises in the public concern cases is that the plaintiff must prove that the defendant acted with *fault*. The type of fault that plaintiff must establish depends on whether the plaintiff is a public or private figure. A public figure is someone who holds public office, or is a candidate for office, or anyone else who enjoys "pervasive fame and notoriety" in public affairs. Kobe Bryant and Julia Roberts are thus public figures, as are Newt Gingrich and Nancy Pelosi.

A public figure plaintiff in a public concern fact pattern must prove that the defendant made the statement in question with *actual malice*. That means that the defendant knew the statement was false when he made it, or was reckless in attempting to verify the accuracy of the statement. In effect, it requires proof that the defendant was deliberately disseminating a lie, or something very close to that. In the Pendleton case, Pendleton would have to show that the newspaper fabricated the story about him taking bribes, or perhaps relied on an anonymous phone call which they made zero effort to verify or investigate.

If the plaintiff in the public concern case is a private figure, the fault requirement can be satisfied by showing that the defendant made the statement negligently. That means that the defendant did not act like a reasonably prudent person in attempting to confirm the accuracy of what was said. In the Pendleton case, let us say that the newspaper story mentions that Pendleton's chief of staff, Pembroke, acted as a "go-between" for the bribes, delivering the envelopes of cash to Pendleton. Pembroke is not likely to be considered a public figure, so he could prevail in his own defamation suit by showing that the newspaper did not act reasonably with regard to the claims it made about him. However, if Pembroke chooses to rely on simple negligence, he would have to prove actual damages—damages would not be presumed. If Pembroke opted to show "actual malice" instead—in other words, the more egregious degree of fault involving intent or recklessness—presumed damages would be permitted.

The point of these elaborate rules is to give speakers some confidence that if they opine on matters of public concern and get something wrong, they are unlikely to be held liable for defamation iso long as it was an honest mistake. You should note that while these rules are only mandatory as a Constitutional matter in the public concern situations, some states have chosen to adopt them for all defamation claims, even those involving purely private parties speaking about matters of purely private concern. In these states—Maryland is an example—every plaintiff must prove at least some fault, and if the fault is not of the malice variety, every plaintiff must prove actual damages as well.

4. The Four Privacy Torts

Privacy law has become a specialized field of law all its own, rather than merely just a topic within the law of torts. Numerous statutes endeavor to protect various aspects of our interest in confidentiality and seclusion. Thus, there are laws that forbid the unauthorized taping of phone conversations, and the unauthorized interception of mail; laws guaranteeing the confidentiality of bank records, and motor vehicle records; and laws that impose various obligations on health care providers to keep information about patients secure. The Constitution of the United States also includes a fundamental privacy protection, namely the right to be free from illegal searches and seizures, and it has also been interpreted to include a more general privacy concept that encompasses the right to obtain various intimate products and services, such as birth control devices and abortions.

As fun as it would be to explore some or all of these topics, they are well beyond the scope of most Torts courses, likely not going to be on your final examination, and thus probably of only modest interest to those who are reading this book. The typical Torts course, if it focuses on privacy at all, limits coverage to the four traditional, common law tort actions designed to vindicate various privacy interests.

The first of these is the tort of *intrusion*. Intrusion is an invasion of the plaintiff's seclusion in a way that would be highly objectionable to the average person. This tort condemns behavior in the nature of spying. Typical types of behavior that would make out a cause of action would include unauthorized wiretapping, eavesdropping or video surveillance. In order to recover, however, the plaintiff must have been in a location where there was a reasonable expectation of privacy, such as his or her home. It is not a tort merely to take the photograph of someone walking on the public street, or to listen in on the conversations of those standing next to you on a subway or city bus.

The second privacy tort is called *disclosure*. This tort is made out by proof of widespread dissemination of confidential information about the plaintiff that would be highly offensive to the average person. The gist of this cause of action is the unauthorized circulation of true, but intimate, personal data about the plaintiff. Thus, it is a tort for the receptionist at your doctor's office to mail copies of your medical chart to everyone who lives in your high rise apartment building. Note that the "widespread dissemination" requirement means that limited circulation of the data would not be actionable—the defendant must distribute the information broadly to a large number of persons.

In addition, there is a newsworthiness exception to this claim. If the information in question is of legitimate public interest, distribution is not tortious. This means that publication of the medical records of a candidate for high public office in the newspaper or on-line is permissible

A somewhat curious cause of action known as *false light* is the third of the traditional privacy torts. This claim requires proof of the widespread dissemination of a material falsehood about the plaintiff that would be highly offensive to the average person. As with the disclosure tort, the widespread dissemination element limits relief to those cases where the defendant has disclosed the inaccurate statement to a significant group of people. The underlying falsehood in a false light fact pattern can be, but need not be, defamatory. In other words, this tort overlaps with defamation, but is somewhat broader. A few states—Florida, New York, Colorado, and Virginia are examples—do not recognize the false light claim, often reasoning that it overlaps too closely with defamation.

A few examples may be helpful. If Drew falsely tells everyone in his apartment building that his neighbor Piper tortures small animals, that would be *both* false light invasion of privacy *and* defamation. In the false light privacy claim, Piper would recover damages for his emotional and social harms, while in the defamation claim he would recover any pecuniary damages he suffered. On the other hand if Drew falsely told everyone that Piper was a Democrat even though he knew that Piper was a Republican, this would not be defamatory, as membership in either major political party is not harmful to reputation (yes, I know you are expecting a lame political joke here, but I will not indulge you). Nonetheless, this misrepresentation would constitute a false light privacy invasion because the mischaracterization of political affiliation is likely to be offensive to most people.

Courts naturally insist that the misrepresentation be fairly significant before they are willing to find the tort of false light to be made out. If Drew had written a biography of Piper and embellished it by adding a false story claiming that Piper spent two weeks in Paris, when in fact Piper had never visited that city, it is unlikely that Piper could recover. Claiming that someone took time off for baguettes and brie on the Champs Elysee is not the kind of falsehood that is likely to be offensive to most folks.

The final privacy cause of action is known as *appropriation*. A claim for appropriation is proved by showing that the defendant made use of defendant's name or likeness for a commercial purpose. Thus, if a defendant uses a photograph of plaintiff on a product package or on a billboard to advertise a product, defendant will be liable (unless, of course, he obtained permission to do so). In order to prevent conflict with the core values of the First Amendment, which protects freedom of expression, the appropriation tort does not reach "newsworthy" uses of others people's name or image. Thus, if a magazine puts a picture of a well-known actress on the cover, in connection with a story about her most recent movie, they do not need permission and their use of her image is not a tort.

Consent is a defense to all of the privacy claims. That certainly makes intuitive sense. If you give someone permission to wiretap your phone, release your medical records, circulate a falsehood about you, or to use your picture on a billboard, you can hardly complain about it. In addition, the various privileges available to defeat a defamation claim will also defeat a claim for false light or disclosure. Thus, if a college professor includes copies of a student transcript along with several hundred letters of recommendation, although this might be widespread dissemination of confidential information, and thus be a prima facie case of the disclosure tort, the professor would have a privilege since the transcript is relevant to his assessment of the student.

5. Nuisance

There are two kinds of nuisance. A private nuisance claim is made out when the owner or occupier of real estate proves that another person has interfered with his ability to use and enjoy his property to an unreasonable degree. Many, but not all, nuisance cases involve inconsistent land use—two parties close-by doing things that are not at all compatible. To take an extreme example, Patterson may operate a clinic for asthma patients on his land, while Dixon, next door, may operate a smoke-belching factory.

A defendant may create a nuisance on purpose, negligently, or without any fault at all, in the case of abnormally dangerous activities. The nature of the defendant's conduct is less important than the resulting harm to the plaintiff. The cases are quite varied. The nuisance can be due to loud noises, foul odors, vibrations, activities that pollute the air, or even visual conditions, like a front yard filled with overgrown weeds and junked cars, that create an eyesore. Sometimes the defendant is being spiteful and sometimes inconsiderate. The conduct that gives rise to a nuisance can overlap with the tort of trespass—for instance, if your neighbor often fires his gun at trees on your property, that would be both a trespass (an intentional physical invasion), and a nuisance—but where the invasion is non-physical (as in the case of noise or smells) the nuisance claim may be the only one available.

A property owner is not entitled to be free from all annoyance. Those on adjacent parcels of land have a right to use their property in a normal fashion and if that is slightly bothersome to neighbors, that is too bad. It is not a nuisance when your neighbor mows his lawn at 9:00 AM on a Sunday, even if you like to sleep late and the noise disturbs you, and it is not a nuisance if he grills hamburgers every Saturday during the summer even though you are a vegan and the smell of those burgers is offensive to you.

Given that we live in a crowded world and all must tolerate some irritation from neighbors, what courts try to do in nuisance cases is strike a balance. They will take into account the nature and characteristics of the neighborhood—is it a quiet suburban cul de sac or an industrial community filled with auto repair shops and small factories? They will consider the utility of the defendant's activities—a defendant who manufactures a life-saving vaccine but who produces offensive odors in the process is less likely to be condemned for creating a nuisance than someone who spitefully burns automobile tires on his front lawn just to annoy his neighbor with the noxious smells. It is very much a fact-specific, case-by-case area of tort law with few hard-and-fast rules to guide the decisions.

Somewhat distinct from the private nuisance situation we have just considered is the so-called "public nuisance." This is an act or course of conduct that causes inconvenience to the public by interfering with some sort of common right. Examples involve activities that interfere with public health, safety or morals, such as obstructing a public street, contaminating a public water supply, or operating a house of prostitution. Many such activities violate statutes, but even if they do not, public officials have a right to sue to abate the nuisance. A private party, however, cannot predicate a claim on a public nuisance unless he has suffered some unique harm that is different from others in the community.

The law of nuisance, with its coverage of such activities as air and water pollution, is considered to be a precursor of modern environmental law. The federal government and the several states have adopted many, quite complex, statutes to deal with activities harmful to the environment. Exploration of environmental law is well beyond the scope of a short and happy treatment of torts. The interested reader should be comforted that there are entire courses (and quite a few lengthy books) devoted to the subject.

6. Business Torts

There are a number of tort claims that can arise out of commercial or business dealings. The two most significant are the claims for fraud and for inducing a breach of contract. Each is fairly intuitive, but elaboration of a few key points will be worthwhile.

A fraud claim will usually arise in the context of a purchase and sale transaction or some other business transaction like the hiring of an employee or the joining of a gym or country club. Although different courts use different lists of elements for fraud we can safely generalize with the following five items: there must be (1) an affirmative misstatement of fact by the defendant; (2) scienter; (3) intent to induce reliance; (4) justifiable reliance; and (5) damage.

The first element requires that the defendant say something inaccurate about the item being sold. For instance, when the seller of a home tells a prospective buyer "we put on a new roof two years ago," when the roof is actually 15 years old, this element is satisfied. The key aspect of this element is that silence cannot be the basis of a fraud claim. If a seller knows that the brakes of his used car are badly in need of repair, but he says nothing about it to a buyer, the buyer will not have a fraud claim.

This is the basis of the classic Latin expression *caveat emptor* or "let the buyer beware," meaning you should not assume a product is in good condition just because nothing has been said to the contrary. To some degree the caveat emptor principle has been displaced by various rules of contract law—particularly the various warranties that will be implied in a sale of goods under the Uniform Commercial Code. It would, however, be perilous for a torts guy to get too deeply into the UCC, so I send you to the *Short and Happy Guide to Contracts* for further details.

The scienter element requires that the defendant make the misstatement either deliberately or recklessly. An honest, or even a negligent error will not expose the seller to a fraud claim. If a seller of real estate tells the buyer that there is no asbestos on the property when in fact there is, the seller would have to prove that the buyer knew about the asbestos and deliberately lied in order to recover for fraud.

The third requirement limits the claim to those persons that the defendant was trying to influence or persuade. Others who may learn of the representations will not have any basis to complain. For instance assume that Darcy, a stockbroker, takes her client Leon to lunch, and tells him that he should buy 1000 shares of Acme Widgets because they are about to secure a patent on a great new product. Further assume that Darcy is making this information up—it is a bald-faced lie. Leon does not buy any Acme stock because he does not have enough cash available, but Pluto, who was sitting nearby at lunch and overheard the conversation does purchase Acme stock. When the stock tanks and Pluto sues Darcy, Pluto will lose. Darcy was not intending to induce *his* reliance on the statement.

The justifiable reliance requirement means that the statement must be material to the transaction and must not be so obviously false or preposterous that a reasonable person would ignore it. Thus if your stockbroker tells you to buy stock in United Airlines because they will begin regular commercial service to the moon next week, you are not likely to be able to win a fraud claim when you buy the stock, wait a week, and discover that there are no flights leaving for the Sea of Tranquility.

The damage requirement for fraud is largely self-explanatory. It often means that the buyer paid more for the item than it was worth, but it could involve other sorts of pecuniary harm. An example from the Restatement is illustrative:

> *A sells to B a machine that he fraudulently misrepresents to be of great value in the manufacture of B's product. B pays the freight of the machine to his factory and expends money in preparing for its installation. On the arrival of the machine the falsity of the representation is discovered and the machine is found to be useless for the purpose for which it was bought. B is entitled to recover, as special damages, the freight that he has paid and the expense that he has incurred in the installation of the machine as well as for harm done to his raw material by the machine before its uselessness was discovered.*

In a case where a party purchases an item in reliance on a fraudulent representation, but the item turns out to be worth *more* than he paid, that party would not have any damages, and would thus not have a claim.

The other economic tort that you may wish to be familiar with is inducing a breach of contract. To prove this claim a plaintiff must show: (1) existence of a valid contract between himself and a third person; (2) knowledge of that contract by the defendant; (3) acts of persuasion by the defendant designed to convince the third person not to perform; (4) breach by the third person; and (5) a showing that the interference or inducement was "improper."

The first two of these elements are, of course self-explanatory. Let us assume that Piper has entered into a contract with Oscar to buy Oscar's house for $300,000 and that Dickens is aware of this contract. The third element would require proof that Dickens approached Oscar and did something to encourage him not to perform. For instance, Dickens might tell Oscar that Piper had bad credit, is disreputable, a terrorist, or something else similarly unsavory. Alternatively, Dickens might just offer Oscar a better deal—for instance he might say "don't sell to Piper, I'll pay you $350,000 if you sell to me." The fourth element is, again, straightforward. Dickens' appeal to Oscar must work—Oscar must refuse to sell the house to Piper.

The final element—that the inducement is improper—is somewhat indefinite. Some individuals are allowed to meddle in contracts and persuade one of the parties not to perform. Typically those who are privileged to do this are advisors or counselors of some sort. For instance, if Dickens is Oscar's accountant and tells him "don't sell to Piper because you will incur a large tax liability; tax rates will be going down next year," Dickens' inducement is not improper and Dickens will not be liable. Similarly, if Dickens is Oscar's father and tells Oscar not to sell because, in his opinion, the house is likely to appreciate in value over the next few years, there would be no liability.

Courts also consider such factors as the defendant's motives, the interests the defendant was seeking to advance, and any social interest in protecting the freedom of action of the defendant in determining if the inducement was improper. Thus if the contract were one which involved some form of lawful but distasteful discrimination, and if the defendant were a civil rights activist who persuaded one party to abandon the contract, a court might find that the motives and social interests weighed against any liability.

CHAPTER XII

Vicarious Liability and Other Miscellaneous Topics

1. Employer Liability for Employee Torts

Sometimes an individual or company can be held liable for a tort even though he or it had no role in causing the injury and did not engage in any tortious conduct. The liability of such a passive party flows from his relationship with the active tortfeasor, who directly perpetrated the wrongful act. The most important relationship that can trigger this kind of liability is the one between an employer and an employee.

Under a principle sometimes called *respondeat superior* an employer is liable for all torts committed by an employee within the scope of employment. Some courts use the labels servant and master for employee and employer, but that smacks a bit too much of hoop skirts and mint juleps for my taste so we will stick with the modern labels. Since most employers have more resources than individual employees, this doctrine is of considerable practical importance to tort victims. It means that if you are run over by a careless FedEx truck driver, you will have a claim not just against the driver, who likely makes a modest income, but against the FedEx Corporation, which in all likelihood has a nice chunk of change in the bank.

The key issue in many cases asserting vicarious liability is resolving the scope of employment issue. In this area courts have developed a rule known as the "frolic and detour" concept, though it actually would be more accurate to call it frolic *or* detour. This principle tells us that when an employee makes a small departure from work-related tasks, he is still acting within the scope of employment. Such small departures are "mere detours." On the other hand, when the departure is more significant, the employee is considered to have left the scope of employment and courts say that he is now "off on a frolic of his own," a phrase which conjures images of the employee skipping merrily off to pursue his own pleasure.

Consider a truck driver instructed to take a load of cargo from Washington to New York City. Obviously, if he carelessly gets into a traffic accident while en route that would unquestionably be within the scope of his employment and his employer would be vicariously liable. Now what if, while en route, he decides to go off the interstate highway and travel 3 miles to his favorite diner, drive-in, or dive in southern New Jersey to get the definitive cheese steak sandwich for lunch and, on this little side trip, he negligently injures someone? In such a case it is likely that a court would hold that this was a "mere detour" and that he was still acting within the scope of his employment.

By way of contrast, if he decided to get off the road and travel 50 miles to Atlantic City to spend a few hours trying his luck at the roulette tables there, a court would surely hold that he was off on a frolic. His employer would not be liable if he got drunk in the casino and carelessly knocked over an old lady standing at one of the slot machines, thereby breaking her hip.

Another common problem that raises scope of employment issues involves *intentional* torts committed by employees. Generally these acts are considered to be outside the scope of employment. Your local supermarket is not likely to be liable when a clerk responds to your question about where to find ketchup with a sharp kick in the groin. This is really only a rough guideline, however, and there are many situations where intentional torts are considered to be within the scope of employment. For instance, here are the facts of one particularly eye-popping Louisiana case:

> *In* LeBrane, *a supervisor became dissatisfied with an employee, fired him, ordered him to leave the workplace and escorted him to the door. The supervisor and LeBrane engaged in a heated argument, which escalated into the supervisor stabbing LeBrane.*[1]

Now that is letting the "good times roll" as they say in New Orleans. In any event, the court held that this stabbing was within the scope of employment because it "was so closely connected in time, place, and causation to his employment-duties as to be regarded a risk of harm fairly attributable to the employer's business."

In the intentional tort cases, courts look to see when and where the tort took place; whether the job is one that involves an authorization to use physical force (like a night club bouncer); and whether the employee was trying to serve the

---

1 *Edmond v. Pathfinder Energy Services, Inc.*, 73 So.3d 424, 426 (La. App. 2011).

employer's purposes when he committed the tort. Like much else in tort law, it is a case-by-case determination not easily reduced to a generalization.

Still another issue that has come up often in the case law involves accidents that occur while an employee is commuting to and from work. For ordinary employees, these are usually considered *outside* the scope of employment. However, where an employee is actually "on the clock" during commuting time—as might be the case with certain workers who must commute a long distance to a remote job site for a period of several months to work on a special project—then the commute is considered job related and any accidents during the commute will trigger vicarious liability on the part of the employer. Relevant factors here include whether the employee is paid for the commuting time, and whether he is using an employer-supplied vehicle or being reimbursed for gas or other expenses of the commute.

2. Independent Contractors

Independent contractors are those hired to perform specific, discrete tasks, such as painters who you might hire to paint your apartment or a plumber who might come to your home to install a new bathtub. A hiring party is *not* vicariously liable for any torts committed by independent contractors. If one of the painters leaves your home to get some more paint and runs down a pedestrian while on the errand, you cannot be held liable.

You can usually identify independent contractors by the fact that they supply their own tools and work largely without supervision—the hiring party does not exercise control over how the work is to be done and has no right to do so. Of course there are many cases where it is hard to distinguish between an independent contractor and an employee. Most courts use a multi-factor test where they throw everything into the pot, taste the stew, and make a decision. The fact that no taxes are withheld; the fact the worker works for multiple parties; the level of skill involved in the task; and the fact that the hiring party is not in business himself are all factors that also point to the "independent contractor" categorization. The nuances are usually explored in depth in a course on "Agency."

The lack of vicarious liability for torts of independent contractors could create some perverse incentives. A business might try to insulate itself from tort liability by not hiring any true employees, but rather attempt to categorize all who work for the enterprise as independent contractors. If successful in such a scheme the business would have no responsibility when a worker injured someone. To avoid this result, there are a number of situations that the courts have labeled "non-delegable duties." These are cases where the hiring party remains liable even though the tortfeasor is an independent contractor. Two of these non-delegable duties are worth a quick note.

First, when the task involves inherently dangerous work, the courts usually invoke the non-delegable duty doctrine to impose vicarious liability on the hiring party. Examples would include such tasks as crop dusting (spraying crops with chemicals from low-flying aircraft) or working with toxic or explosive substances such as acids or fireworks.

The other important instance of a non-delegable duty arises when the victim of the independent contractor's carelessness is a person lawfully on the hiring party's land. In these cases, the hiring party is usually a business of some kind, which has hired someone to come on the property to do renovations and repairs. If the contractor's negligence injures a customer, the business owner is vicariously liable for that. The Restatement gives the example of a plumber (an independent contractor), hired by a hotel, who negligently installs a cold water faucet in a shower so that a guest at the hotel is burned. In that case, the plumber is directly liable and the hotel is vicariously liable. This gives the scalded guest a choice of defendants.

Of course, if a party hires an incompetent independent contractor, that can be a ground for liability as well, but the liability in such a case is not vicarious. If the Deerfield Mall wants to hire a contractor to come in and water the various potted plants it has placed in boxes along railings at the mall, and it chooses to hire Stoner Plant Maintenance, a company where most of the workers are known by the mall management to use marijuana heavily, Deerfield will be liable when a stoned worker drops one of the potted plants on the head of a shopper. This is a simple case of negligent hiring, and should not be confused with vicarious liability.

3. Other Potential Vicarious Liability Scenarios

In some states, the owner of an automobile who lends his car to another can be held vicariously liable for any torts the driver may commit. This rule is sometimes called the "permissive use" doctrine. Under a variation of this principle, known as the "family car doctrine" there will be vicarious liability only if the driver and the owner are members of the same household. The majority rule, however, is that car-owners are *not* vicariously liable for the torts of drivers, even if the driver has permission to use the car or is a member of the owner's family.

Bear two points in mind about the automobile situation, however. First, the owner can be liable *for his own negligence* in letting the other person drive. Thus, if you give the keys of your car to a drunk, you will surely be held liable. Second, in the so-called "real world" most automobile owners have liability insurance. Indeed, they are required to have such insurance by law and proof of insurance is usually necessary to register the car. The typical insurance policy covers torts committed by any authorized driver. So even in states where the owner is not vicariously liable, a victim carelessly hit by someone driving with permission is likely to be able to tap the owner's insurance in a suit against the driver.

Much to the surprise of some, parents are not vicariously liable for the torts of their children. They can, as we discussed in the chapter on Duty in the law of negligence, sometimes be liable for a their own negligence in failing to supervise, and they can also be liable for their own negligence in entrusting a dangerous instrumentality to the child if a reasonable person would not have done so. Absent parental negligence, however, the victim's only claim will be against the child. If that seems either silly or unfortunate to you because suing a 9-year-old for his milk money is not likely to yield much of a recovery, bear in mind that children are often covered parties under homeowner's liability insurance policies.

4. Wrongful Death and Survival Statutes

While it comes as a surprise to most modern lawyers and law students, under traditional common law rules, a tort claim could not be pursued if the victim of the tort died. Neither the victim's estate, nor surviving family members, who might have been deprived of support and left grief-stricken, had any recourse. This is the source of one of the oldest and grimmest attempts at humor in torts—that if you carelessly run someone over it is in your interest to back up and run him over again. The "joke" being that if you killed the poor fellow you would not owe any damages.

By the late 19th century various states began overturning this rule by legislation. This legislation usually involved two separate provisions—a survival statute and a wrongful death statute. A survival statute allows the estate of a deceased tort victim to pursue a claim. In this claim the estate can recover any damages that the victim could have recovered up to the time of death. Thus, if a person is injured by a tort in February, and dies in May, the estate could recover for any medical bills incurred during that 3-month interval, any wages that would have been earned during that 3-month interval, and for the pain and suffering during that 3-month interval. Where death is instantaneous, the recovery available in a survival claim is likely to be modest because there is no interval between injury and death in which the victim incurs costs or suffers pain. Note that the survival action would be available no matter what tort is involved. The estate of a victim of a shooting—a battery—would have such a claim; so would the estate of a victim of a drunk driver (negligence) or the estate of someone killed by a defective product (strict liability).

The other statute that modifies the common law is known as a "wrongful death" statute. It grants an entirely new cause of action to a dead victim's surviving family members. There are two principal item of recovery available in this kind of suit. The first is for loss of support during what would have been the period of the victim's remaining ordinary life span. In some states the measure of damages is simply the amount the victim would have earned minus what he would have spent on his own personal support. In others, the wrongful death plaintiffs may actually have to show how much support they likely would have received, and for how long. Second, most states now allow recovery for a variety of emotional consequences of the death such as sorrow and sadness, along with compensation for loss of companionship (in the case of a spouse) or guidance (in the case of a child).

There are two very important notes about wrongful death litigation. First—wrongful death is not the name of a tort. It is the name of a cause of action, or a procedural device. If someone says they are suing "for wrongful death," the next question should be "and what tort are you suing for?" If your spouse is shot you can bring a wrongful death claim for battery. If your spouse is crushed by a steel beam that was negligently attached to a construction crane you can bring a wrongful death claim for negligence. If your spouse is killed by a runaway car with defective steering you can bring a wrongful death claim alleging strict product liability. If your spouse is eaten by a tiger you can bring a wrongful death claim for strict liability due to the keeping of wild animals. You get the point. Wrongful death is not a substantive tort.

Second, a wrongful death claim is "derivative." Any defenses that could have been asserted against the decedent—the direct victim—can be raised against the surviving family members in the wrongful death suit. These might include things like consent or self-defense if the underlying substantive claim is an intentional tort or comparative negligence if the underlying claim is negligence.

5. Loss of Consortium

Whenever the victim of a tort—any tort—is a married person, his or her uninjured spouse also gets a separate cause of action against all the same defendants. This cause of action is known as the loss of consortium claim. It is designed to compensate the plaintiff-spouse for three types of harm.

First, it permits a recovery for loss of the household services that would have been performed by the injured spouse, but for the tort. For instance, if the injured spouse normally prepared meals, cleaned the home, or took care of the lawn, the uninjured consortium plaintiff can recover money because these tasks are now not getting done. Second, a consortium plaintiff can recover for "loss of society." This is essentially a recovery for loss of companionship. The idea is that because of the injury to the other party in the marriage, the consortium plaintiff is lonely, has no one with whom to enjoy the pleasures of life, and is generally morose. Finally, the consortium plaintiff can also recover for the loss of sexual intimacy during the period of the injured spouse's illness and recovery.

These items of damage are not awarded automatically. A consortium plaintiff must prove them. In other words, it is not assumed that the spouses help each other around the house, are companionable, or have a physical relationship. If the marriage is strained and the spouses have been living in separate bedrooms and barely talking to each other, there will be little if any recovery for loss of consortium.

In some states, the consortium concept has been expanded to other relationships beyond marriage. In these jurisdictions, an uninjured child might recover for a tortious injury inflicted on a parent (loss of parental consortium), or conversely, the parent might recover for an injury to a child (loss of filial consortium). Of course, the damages recoverable in such claims, where they are allowed, are adjusted in light of the relationship. The majority of states have been hesitant to recognize these additional categories of consortium claims for fear of multiplying claims and imposing crushing liability based on a single tortious act. For instance, if a careless driver hits a pedestrian who is married with five children, the driver could be liable to all seven members of that family for the single act of carelessness. While one or two damage awards might seem appropriate, many states feel that six or seven is a tad excessive.

It is important to note that like wrongful death claims, all consortium suits are "derivative." That means that any defense that can be asserted against the direct victim can also be asserted against the consortium plaintiff. If Harry is run down by a drunk driver after jaywalking, in his suit against the driver, his recovery will be reduced by his comparative negligence. That means that if his wife Wanda brings a consortium claim against that same drunk driver, her recovery will be similarly reduced. If Henry sues Draper for a battery in connection with a punch in the nose and Draper can prove he acted in self-defense, that will defeat not only Henry's battery claim, but his wife Wilma's consortium claim as well.